ALL 92
AND THE TREBLE

ALL 92

AND THE TREBLE

92 League Grounds, One Season, while witnessing
Manchester City's Triumphant Treble

ROBERT LEE

Troubador Publishing Ltd
Unit E2 Airfield Business Park
Harrison Road, Market Harborough
Leicestershire LE16 7UL
Tel: 0116 279 2299
Email: books@troubador.co.uk
Web: www.troubador.co.uk

ISBN 978-1-83628-006-4

British Library Cataloguing in Publication Data.
A catalogue record for this book is available from the British Library.

Printed and bound by CPI Group (UK) Ltd, Croydon, CR0 4YY
Typeset in 11pt Minion Pro by Troubador Publishing Ltd, Leicester, UK

MIX
Paper | Supporting
responsible forestry
FSC
www.fsc.org
FSC® C013604

To all football fans up and down the country who give this sport its unique atmosphere by spending their hard earned cash to follow their team through thick and thin, in all weathers and conditions.

Contents

Foreword

This book started out as a narrative of a project I had set myself, which was to visit a match at each of the 92 football league grounds in one season – an objective I named 'Project 92'. I was a bit stuck for a title. 'All 92' sounded dull and a bit vague. But as the season progressed it became apparent that Manchester City, the team I have supported for over 70 years, could be on the verge of something special. And so it came to pass in June 2023 that, on a memorable night at the Ataturk Olympic Stadium in Istanbul, City beat Inter Milan to win the Champions League for the first time, and thus complete a historic treble.

So I have woven the narrative of Manchester City's season into the story of my journey round the country, which took me to grounds from Accrington to Wycombe.

And 'All 92' has morphed into 'All 92 – and the Treble'.

I hope you enjoy the journey.

Acknowledgements

My grateful thanks are due to the following who helped me to visit matches at their home clubs, either by loaning me friends/relatives' season tickets or facilitating buying tickets:

David Carrington, Andrew Christophers, Neil Cottrell, John de Pear, Danny Dyer, Julian Ellis, Ray Grainger, Dan Jacobs, Dave Lawrence, and particularly to John Newman, whose generosity was poorly rewarded as he picked up a speeding ticket as he drove us home.

Also to John, mine host of the Castle Inn in Accrington whose unsolicited generosity I've acknowledged in the narrative.

The Challenge – Why and How

I had for a long time had a notion of visiting all 92 league grounds, and this crystallised when in 2021 I found myself single and living on my own for the first time in 45 years. The challenge I set myself was to attend a match at each of the grounds within the 2022/3 season. I didn't confine myself to league fixtures, but they all had to be first team matches – no reserve games, no friendlies.

I also wanted to take the opportunity to raise a bit of money for two charities I support – Emmaus Lambeth, a branch of the worldwide organisation for the homeless, and Daisy's Dream, which provides bereavement counselling for young people.

The 2022/23 season represented a unique opportunity as it was lengthened by the Qatar World Cup. I was determined not to let the project dominate my life completely, and scheduled a couple of two week holidays, plus a Christmas break. This left me 41 weeks so I was committing to an average of over two matches a week. Scheduling presented quite a challenge, especially as many top matches have their dates/times moved at quite short notice for television. And as the season went on, I had fewer unwatched matches to choose from. I took advantage of a couple of European matches and was always on the lookout for cup replays. Getting tickets wasn't generally a problem, though it usually involved registering with the club. As a result my inbox would fill up with endless offers on merchandising.

I had invaluable help, for which I'm eternally grateful, from several friends who had season tickets or contacts, and I only had to resort to secondary ticket websites three times – for Old Trafford and the two Liverpool venues. I won't embarrass the site by naming it, but the customer service was excellent. I was given a number to phone in the event of any problems – 'whatever you do, don't approach a steward'!

As an adjunct to watching football, I wanted to improve my knowledge of my country, and I put quite a lot of effort into visiting sites of interest such as museums. I was also able to do some family history research, as my father was born in Carlisle, my mother in Rochdale, and my maternal grandparents lived in both Blackburn and Burnley.

My general plan was to travel by rail to anywhere north of Birmingham or west of Bristol. But this wasn't always possible as the season was marred by a succession of rail strikes. It's surprising how far you can do a round trip on a Saturday for a 3pm kick-off – Plymouth, Morecambe, Hull. I used a variety of hotels and pubs for overnight stays, most often for Tuesday/Wednesday matches.

An added bonus to the season was the historic success of the club I have supported for over 70 years – Manchester City. The first match I watched was when my father took me in September 1952, a 1-0 defeat to West Bromwich Albion (scorer Ronnie Allen if you're interested). I have followed them ever since through thick and thin (for about 30 years mostly thin), so have included an account of their season as a backdrop to this narrative. So please indulge me if, to avoid repetition, I sometimes refer to the team as just 'City' or, since I identify with them so closely, occasionally as 'we'.

I have a secondary support for Brentford, as I've lived in West London all my working life, and spent many happy hours on the terraces at Griffin Park with my children when they were growing up. None of them has adopted Manchester City. Tim, who lives in Barcelona, supports Crystal Palace. He has made a career in football as a freelance producer and TV commentator on La Liga. His brothers Nick and Adam support Arsenal, and are hoping that 2023/24 is the year that their team dethrones City. For completeness, I should add that my stepson Neil supports Nottingham Forest, and my daughter Katharine has played a little recreationally.

The third team which I follow is Hampton and Richmond Borough, who play in the National League South five minutes' walk from where I live.

The game has evolved dramatically since I first watched. Tackling was much more robust and you could charge the goalkeeper outside the goal area. (Indeed, that was the raison d'etre of the goal area – defining where a goal kick can be taken was secondary.) The balls were sodden, dementia-inducing lumps, and pitches were a mud bath from autumn onwards. Players wore shirts numbered 1 to 11. Before transistor radios and smart phones, half time scores were promulgated by putting numbers up on a board. And, before television called the shots, the interval was only 10 minutes. The back pass rule wasn't introduced until 1990, and it was common for a team to start a match with a series of passes to the goalkeeper 'so he could get a feel for the ball'. (I was told that Fulham once contrived to score an own goal doing this, but that might be an urban myth). And there were no substitutes till 1967 – injured players would hobble on the wing unless they'd broken a leg.

Almost 71 years after my first visit to Maine Road, these were the 92 matches which I watched.

1. Watford v Sheffield United

1 August 2022 – Vicarage Road – EFL Championship

I normally consider August to be the cricket season, but this project meant swallowing my principles and the first of the month saw me head off to Watford for the televised Monday night game. Despite being in its centenary year, Vicarage Road is a bright and cheerful stadium with its red and yellow colour scheme, and I had a good seat in the Graham Taylor Stand, where I was spotted on TV by some viewers with a keen eye.

Watford, just relegated, had a new manager, Rob Edwards from Forest Green Rovers – a change from their usual practice of hiring and firing old hands. They were the deserved winner of this match between two promotion candidates. Captained by Tom Cleverley, they squandered a couple of early chances, as did Sheffield United. Watford's winner came in the 56th minute, when they counter attacked after a corner and the Brazilian Joao Pedro scored from Ismaili Sarr's cross. Emmanuel Dennis and Sama were a handful and I felt that if Watford hung onto them they'd make a challenge for promotion.

The match day experience was somewhat tarnished by 50 minutes gridlock on leaving the nearby multi-storey car park.

Watford 1 Sheffield United 0 (Joao Pedro 56)
Attendance 19,536

2. West Ham United v Manchester City

7 August 2022 – London Stadium – Premier League

The first weekend of the Premier League season was the hottest of the year, the only time I have gone to an English league match in tee-shirt and shorts. Outside the London Stadium, of which West Ham are only the tenants, concessionaires were charging up to £7.30 a pint for lager, inside 'only' £6.10. The stadium capacity had been increased, so the crowd of over 62,000 was a club record.

It was my very first sight of Erling Haaland, who had had indifferent reviews for his performance in the Community Shield the previous week. First impression – my god, he's huge! Not only huge, but quick. After an initial flourish from West Ham, Haaland burst onto a shrewd through pass from Gundogan and was felled by the West Ham keeper Areola, who had just replaced the injured Fabianski. Haaland calmly rolled home the penalty, and then celebrated by sitting down in the zen position – a posture which was to become familiar as the season progressed. In the second half he was put through again, this time by De Bruyne and scored comfortably. I was in the away end, where fans amused themselves by singing to Haaland's father Alf-Inge in one of the boxes to our left, and hurling abuse at the media centre, directed at Roy Keane whose well documented tackle had ended Alfie's career.

It was a comfortable win to start City's title defence. Alan Shearer, who holds the Premier League record with 260 goals, simply tweeted '258 to go'.

West Ham United 0 Manchester City 2 (Haaland 36 p, 65)

Attendance 62,433

3. West Bromwich Albion v Watford

8 August 2022 – The Hawthorns – EFL Championship

My second Monday Night Football match took me to watch Watford again, this time at The Hawthorns. The stadium, which has been modernised several times since being built in 1900, lies just by a junction of the M5, and is the highest ground in the football league at 550 feet above sea level.

Twelve minutes after the start, I'd probably already seen my goal of the season. Against the run of play, after the Watford goalkeeper had made a couple of good saves, Senegalese international Ismaila Sarr picked up a ball in front of me in the centre circle, just inside his own half, turned, and with barely a glance up, spotted the WBA keeper off his line, and lobbed him from 55 yards. A quite superb strike, without even a preliminary touch. WBA continued to enjoy good possession and this paid off when they equalised in first half stoppage time. After 71 minutes Sarr was brought down in the area. But he is clearly better from 55 yards than from 12, as his weak penalty was easily saved and the match finished 1-1.

As it happened, having watched Watford twice in my first three matches, I never saw them again. They reverted to type by sacking manager Rob Edwards in late September, appointing Slavan Bilic and also getting rid of him in March.

The beneficiaries of Edwards being fired were Luton Town, and Watford finished 11th.

WBA 1 (Grant 45+2) Watford 1 (Sarr 12)

Attendance 22,365

4. Oxford United v Swansea City

9 August 2022 – Kassam Stadium – Carabao Cup Round 1

I stayed overnight in West Bromwich and, before this match, I spent a delightful afternoon at Kenilworth Castle, one of England's finest, with much still standing. Almost exactly 900 years old, it was subjected to a six month siege, one of the longest in English history in 1266. In the 16th century it was owned by Robert Dudley, Earl of Leicester, and Queen Elizabeth visited him there on many occasions, with lavish feasting and, historians speculate, possibly other activities.

A contrast to the old Manor Ground, The Kassam Stadium is odd. As the club is planning yet another stadium in 2026, this one is unfinished, with only three sides built! The fourth end looks out over a car park and shopping centre.

This first round Carabao Cup match produced an upset with Oxford United from League One beating Swansea City from the division above. This looked unlikely for a long time. Swansea took an early lead when the Oxford keeper handled outside his area (lucky to get yellow not red) and midfielder Jay Fulton thumped in the free kick. They doubled their lead after 25 minutes and looked safe for a win. But 18 minutes from time, the Oxford striker Gorrin scored by charging down a clearance, and they equalised deep into stoppage time when a free kick took a massive deflection. No extra time, straight to penalties

– a good idea for a midweek evening match. Swansea's fourth penalty was saved onto the crossbar, and Oxford converted their fifth to go through.

That was the end of their giant killing though – they went out at home against Crystal Palace in the next round.

Oxford United 2 (Gorrin 72, Brannagan 90+3)
Swansea 2 (Fulton 8, Cullen 25)
Oxford won 5-3 on penalties.

Attendance 4,373

5. Crawley Town v Northampton Town

13 August 2022 – Broadfield Stadium – League Two

My first venture into League Two was fairly local, at the Broadfield Stadium on the outskirts of Crawley, which was built in 1997, and then upgraded in 2012 when Crawley Town achieved promotion to the Football League. It has a pleasant bar outside the ground which was ideal for refreshments on a balmy summer evening.

Coming into the match, Crawley had one point from three matches to Northampton's seven. Crawley took an early lead with a neat goal from about six yards. The scorer was James Balagizi, who was on loan from Liverpool. Northampton soon equalised through their midfielder Sam Hoskins, who was making his 300th appearance. Ten minutes later Hoskins scored again, this time from a curling free kick which should probably have been saved. Midway through the second half, Balagizi scored again to level the match and, with a longish drive home looming, I left a couple of minutes early to beat the traffic. As I reached my car there was a loud, but muted, roar. It came from the away supporters as substitute Kieron Bowie scored the winner from a Hoskins pass.

**Crawley Town 2 (Balagizi 4, 68) Northampton 3
(Hoskins 13, 23, Bowie 90+2)
Attendance 2,472**

6. Stevenage FC v Peterborough United

23 August 2022 – Lamex Stadium – Round 2 Carabao Cup

Another evening match within driving distance. In the afternoon I visited Berkhamsted en route, and had a walk round the castle, or what's left of it. Berkhamsted was where William the Conqueror received the English surrender after the Battle of Hastings, and the castle was later occupied by Thomas Becket.

From there it was a short drive to Stevenage's Lamex Stadium, just off the A1(M). Built in the 1960s, the ground had a substantial upgrade to be fit for the Football League when Stevenage were promoted in 2010. It's a ground with only basic facilities – no programmes, no alcohol!

As in the previous week's Carabao match, the home side were playing a team from the division above, and both sides were standing second in their division. Stevenage had won at Championship club Reading with a late goal in the first round. Peterborough United from League One, managed by Sir Alex Ferguson's son Darren, brought over 500 fans with them.

The disparity in the rankings of the teams wasn't obvious during the match, which featured several good chances at either end. Peterborough's Ricky Jade-Jones, a speedy and tricky forward, particularly caught my eye. They had a goal chalked off for offside in the second half and, five minutes from full time, there was a goalmouth scramble when it seemed that Peterborough must score, but the Stevenage defence held firm.

Just when I was resigning myself to another penalty shootout and late drive home, a low ball into the area landed at the feet of Stevenage's Jamie Reid, and he placed his shot wide of the goalkeeper to send his team into the third round. Joyful scenes followed, and it was hard not to feel sorry for the Peterborough players and fans. This was the first time in their history Stevenage had progressed so far, but they subsequently went out to Charlton on penalties in the third round.

Stevenage FC 1 (Reid 90+3) Peterborough United 0

Attendance 2,292

7. Leeds United v Barnsley

24 August 2022 – Elland Road – Round 2 Carabao Cup

My next match at Leeds coincided with Ukraine Independence Day, and the city centre was livened up with many attractive Ukrainian ladies decked out in blue and yellow, doing some fundraising to which I was delighted to contribute.

This was my first visit to the famous Elland Road Stadium, which originally opened in 1897. Its stands are a reminder of the club's great past, being named after John Charles, Don Revie, Jack Charlton and Norman Hunter. My ticket in the John Charles Stand cost only £11.

As is commonplace for Premier League teams in the Carabao Cup, Leeds made 10 changes, and the only two players I'd heard of, Llorente and Cooper, were substituted at half time. They were still far too strong for Barnsley, who didn't help themselves by missing a penalty at 1-2. My eye was soon caught by Luis Sinisterra, a talented Colombian who Leeds had signed from Feyenoord for £21 million, who gave Leeds the lead after 21 minutes with a fine shot from 20 yards. Just after the half hour, Sinisterra was brought down in the area and Polish international Mateusz Klich doubled the lead from the penalty spot. Leeds were threatening to run away with the tie but Barnsley pulled one back with a clever header from a free kick, and then missed the chance to draw level when, having won a penalty, they hit the post from the penalty spot.

Sinisterra set up Klich to score a third goal for Leeds with a curling shot shortly after half time, and the game then expired gently in a plethora of substitutions. I was not surprised to see Sinisterra win his first cap for Colombia a couple of months later.

The following morning before my train back to London, I had time to visit the Royal Armouries Museum, which is reached with a pleasant walk along the River Aire, and houses Britain's fine collection of armaments through the ages.

Leeds United 3 (Sinisterra 21, Klich 32 p, 56)
Barnsley 1 (Andersen 35)

Attendance 35,472

8. Luton Town v Sheffield United

26 August 2022 – Kenilworth Road – EFL Championship

Presumably because of the high attendance anticipated, Luton wouldn't sell me a ticket until two days before the match. My first impressions of Kenilworth Road were not helped by the fact that the car park recommended by the club website, while free, was over a mile away. The walk there is not the most scenic and takes you through a housing estate. A fellow spectator at a subsequent match claimed that, while en route to a match there, he had helped someone hang out their washing.

Sheffield were top of the table, unbeaten since I saw them lose their opener at Watford. Their squad included two Manchester City academy players on loan – midfielder James McAtee and Tommy Doyle, who can claim not one but two ex City grandfathers, Mick Doyle and Glyn Pardoe. The two loanees played a half each.

In general during the season, my fellow spectators were enthusiastic and often knowledgeable, but on that evening I had the misfortune to be behind a guy who must have had a bad week. Every other minute he would leap to his feet, veins on his forehead bulging like Roy Keane in his heyday confronting a referee, yelling a stream of adjectivally monotonous invective at the opposition or an official.

Luton took an early lead with a powerful header but Sheffield's Scottish international Oli McBurnie equalised in the second half with a volley at the back post. Shortly before the end Luton's Cameron Jerome drew a finger-tip save from the Sheffield goalkeeper, but the match ended 1-1 and Sheffield stayed on top of the table.

Luton Town 1 (Morris 10) Sheffield United 1 (McBurnie 56)
Attendance 9,882

9. Aston Villa v West Ham United

28 August 2022 – Villa Park – Premier League

The traffic was inevitably heavy for this Sunday 2pm kick-off. I was worried about parking, but a Seventh Day Adventist church was flogging spaces for £5 only 15 minutes' walk from the ground, the walk taking me past the famous Holte pub, which, at over 150 years, is even older than the stadium.

West Ham arrived at this fixture not only pointless after three matches, but also without even having scored a goal – a sequence which I felt was due to end. Villa had the ball in the net early on following a corner, but the ball was ruled to have gone out of play first. The match livened up a bit after half time when David Moyes brought on Benrahma. Lucas Digne made a brilliant tackle to deny Bowen when he was through on goal. Then with 14 minutes to go, Declan Rice played a through pass to Pablo Fornals whose speculative shot from outside the area took a wicked deflection for the decisive goal. Bowen narrowly failed to double the lead near the end. Happiness for the substantial army of West Ham fans, boos from the Villa supporters. Steven Gerrard's shine was wearing off.

Major developments are planned for Villa Park, a grand old stadium.

Aston Villa 0, West Ham United 1 (Fornals 74)
Attendance 41,796

10. Burnley v Millwall

30 August 2022 – Turf Moor – EFL Championship

Burnley, situated on the edge of the moors, is a nicer town than I remembered and features in my family history. My grandmother was born just up the road in Padiham, where her father had a tobacconist shop, and she married my grandfather in St Mary's Catholic Church, literally a stone's throw from Turf Moor, which is also next door to Burnley Cricket Club, where England legend James Anderson learned his trade. Burnley's home since 1883, it is the second oldest ground in the football league. My walk to the stadium also took me past a pub named the Lord Dyche after the manager who had won them promotion. Though I chose the nearby Wetherspoons where beer was £2.19 a pint.

Sean Dyche left after Burnley had been relegated the previous season, and Manchester City legend Vincent Kompany had taken over. Burnley also had City academy defender Taylor Harwood-Bellis as a loan player.

I had a good seat in the Bob Lord Stand. Burnley were generally on top, though the main threats at either end in the first half came from free kicks. In the second half, Brazilian full back Vitinho put Burnley ahead with a neat goal at the far post, and ten minutes later Jay Rodriguez sealed the three points scoring from close range after the Millwall keeper parried a shot to his feet.

The following morning I was able to find a couple of houses where my grandparents had spent their early married life.

Burnley 2 (Vitinho 62, Rodriguez 72), Millwall 0
Attendance 18,372

11. Stoke City v Swansea City

31 August 2022 – Bet365 Stadium – EFL Championship

Arriving at the station one is reminded of Stoke's industrial heritage as the capital of the Potteries by a statue of Josiah Wedgwood. It was a pleasant half hour walk to the ground, along the banks of the Trent and Mersey canal, which was constructed in the 18th century to facilitate the exports of ceramics from the area.

The football industry is massively in hock to the gambling industry, no club more so than Stoke City, which is owned by billionaire Denise Coates, who has turned Bet365 into a leader in the online gaming market. The stadium which bears her company's name was opened in 1997 as the Britannia Stadium. The official opening was carried out by Sir Stanley Mathews and, after his death in 2002, his ashes were buried under the centre circle.

My seat was so central that I literally had one foot in each half. Swansea had an early escape when they made a mess of a short goal kick. A long range lob hit the bar with the keeper way out of position, and he scrambled back just in time to claw away the follow up. But Swansea took the lead with their first attack when Dutch striker Joel Piroe turned in a cross from short range.

They held onto their lead for most of the match, with Stoke missing several good chances. Liam Delap, on loan from Manchester City, almost scored just before the end, and then in stoppage time substitute Tyrese Campbell, son of Kevin, bundled home the equaliser. A valuable point for Stoke in Alex Neil's first match in charge after leaving Sunderland.

Stoke City 1 (Campbell 90+1) Swansea City 1 (Piroe 6)
Attendance 18,697

12. Brighton & Hove Albion v Leicester City

4 September 2022 – Amex Stadium – Premier League

It was a lovely early September Sunday afternoon and my seat in the Amex Stadium had a lovely view of the South Downs.

Leicester had only managed one point in August, but they took an early lead. Solly March lost possession, and some quick passing gave Iheanacho a short range tap in. March made amends a few minutes later when his back post header cannoned in off the Leicester defender. Brighton then took the lead with a superb strike from Moses Caicedo from a tight angle. The home side were dominating the play, but they conceded an equaliser when Dunk made a hash of a long clearance.

The second half began with a spectacular 35 yard strike from Alexis MacAllister after a corner was cleared. After a full minute it became apparent that there was a VAR review. A full four minutes after the shot, the goal was chalked off for a marginal offside. During this time, spectators in the ground without access to the radio commentary were totally in the dark. Brighton weren't denied the lead for long though. Another excellent move involving MacAllister and Pascal Gross ended with a fine shot across Ward from Leondre Trossard. MacAllister then added two more goals – a penalty after Trossard was tripped, and then in stoppage time a brilliant free kick. It was to be a memorable season for the Argentine international with the un-Hispanic surname, as he went on to collect a World Cup winners medal and complete a high profile transfer to Liverpool.

Meanwhile the knives were out for Brendan Rodgers.

**Brighton & HA 5 (Thomas og 10, Caicedo 15,
Trossard 64, MacAllister 71 p, 90+7)
Leicester City 2 (Iheanacho 1, Daka 33)
Attendance 31,185**

13. Rochdale v Leyton Orient

My next match had been booked at AFC Wimbledon the following Saturday, but a more important event intervened. The Queen died. All league football was postponed at the weekend, so there was a 9 day gap before I took the train north. By reputation Rochdale, just north of Manchester, is one of the poorest towns in England and its reputation is further tainted by the grooming scandal. But a century ago it was a thriving town, with its mills contributing to the Lancashire cotton industry. It also has family connections for me. My grandfather was in the clothing trade, and after their marriage in Burnley in 1910, my grandparents moved to Haslingden and then, in 1914, to Rochdale, where three of their daughters were born, including the youngest, my mother. In addition, at the end of World War 2, my family lived in Castleton, which is just above Rochdale on the moors, until I was aged two – an event of which of course I have no memory.

So on arrival in Rochdale, I sought out the house in Sparthfield Avenue where my grandparents had lived – a small late Victorian or Edwardian terraced house in good condition. To get a wider angle for a photo I stepped across the road. A young man was sitting on the step of the house opposite who engaged me in conversation and offered me a drink, which I declined. He was with an older woman, his mother I assume. I explained what I was doing there and he immediately translated into Urdu for her. I asked him how long he'd lived there, and he pointed to his mother and said that she'd been there over thirty years. 'Thirty years and you still don't speak any English' I said to her pleasantly. She looked completely blank. It brought home to me how difficult it must be for the older generation of immigrants – especially women – to be so cut off from the culture of the country they have come to.

Spotland is just on the outskirts of the town. It has one of the odder names of old league grounds, but now it goes by the less glamorous name of the Crown Oil Arena. To give them great credit, the club produced a splendid programme featuring the late Queen.

The match featured top against bottom, with Leyton Orient only having dropped two points, and Rochdale only having won two. The match was unmemorable. Leyton were much the better team but had to be content with one goal, scored by George Moncur, son of former Swindon and West Ham player John, in the 35th minute. The game was drifting so I snuck out after 88 minutes to try and get an Uber before the rush. I had just left when there was a big roar. A Rochdale equaliser? It was loud, but not sustained enough for that. The explanation was a penalty to Rochdale. But it was saved! I wondered if that would matter at the end of the season. (It didn't).

The following morning I walked up to Castleton and located the unpretentious semi where I lived in 1946. Then I took the local train to Manchester for my next match, which would be up a gear – the Champions League.

Rochdale 0 Leyton Orient 1 (Moncur 35)
Attendance 2,173

14. Manchester City v Borussia Dortmund

14 September 2022 – Etihad Stadium – Champions League

This was in the second round of group matches, City having started well with a 4-0 win away at Sevilla. While both teams were likely to qualify, finishing top of the group makes the next round draw more advantageous. My walk from my hotel near Piccadilly to the Etihad was held up by a massive police presence where the main road crosses the Ashton Canal. Looking back down Ancoats Road, I could see a large group marching towards us. A demonstration? No, it was the Dortmund supporters getting a police escort to the ground! Once inside, the produced the most sustained two hours of chanting I've ever heard. They were to my left, and their cheerleader stood facing them on a front row seat to conduct them. He never watched a ball kicked.

It was the first game against his old club for Haaland and also for Manuel Akanji, who had joined a few weeks earlier on deadline day. City were probably the better team in the first half without making any clear chances, but early in the second half they fell behind to an excellent headed goal from Jude Bellingham. Guardiola responded with a triple substitution, bringing on Foden, Silva and Alvarez for Gundogan, Mahrez and Grealish. Not a bad bench to have! The team immediately picked up the pace and looked more threatening. Haaland hit a post from De Bruyne's through pass and then Stones equalised with a powerful swerving shot from outside the area. Six minutes from time, Haaland scored an acrobatic winner. It was at the far end from me, and all I saw was a blur of limbs. It was only when watching a replay later that I could appreciate the athleticism and skill of his 'kung fu' kick, and the subtlety of Cancelo's outside of the foot pass.

In the pub later the Dortmund supporters sang heartily and agreed City were the better team.

Manchester City 2 (Stones 80, Haaland 84)
Borussia Dortmund 1 (Bellingham 56)
Attendance 50,441

15. Cambridge United v Barnsley

17 September 2022 – Abbey Stadium – League One

My next match was a day trip to Cambridge United. They were a non-league club when I was at university there, but were elected to the League in 1970 and, under the management of Ron Atkinson, briefly made it to the second tier where they achieved a highest position of 7th. I had an introduction through a friend to one of their directors, and he joined me for a brief chat after he'd fulfilled his social obligation to have lunch with the visiting board members. He explained that the club had purchased the Abbey Stadium and planned to expand it to hold 12,000. But he wasn't sanguine about their chances that day, thinking that ex championship team Barnsley would be stronger.

He was right. Although Cambridge hit a post early on, Barnsley scored first after some sloppy defending, and then doubled their lead with a looping header after 76 minutes. A 90th minute goal secured the win and lifted Barnsley above Cambridge into 6th place. The match can't have gripped my attention too much, as it wasn't till the next day I realised that Barnsley had played the last 20 minutes a man short after defender Liam Kitching had picked up a second yellow card. There were 14 minutes added time after a horrible injury to the Cambridge goalkeeper which looked like a broken nose.

If Cambridge is planning a capacity increase, it will want to attract a larger share of the student market, in which case they might want to reconsider their no alcohol policy!

Cambridge United 0 Barnsley 3
(Cole 24, Cundy 76, Norwood 90)
Attendance 6,138

16. Peterborough United v Port Vale

24 September 2022 – Weston Homes Stadium
(London Road) – League One

The following week I had a Friday night dinner at my old Cambridge college, so visiting Peterborough on the Saturday was a natural choice. En route I visited the 14th century Longthorpe Tower, which has some splendid wall paintings. Peterborough itself was in festive mood, with lots of people in costume and Morris dancing type activities, and I spent some time in the Cathedral. Katherine of Aragon buried there but Henry VII wouldn't fund a memorial for her.

So in 1893 the *Daily Mail* raised the money for one by getting a penny from every reader called Katherine – my daughter's name!

The century old London Road ground, now sponsored by Weston Homes Stadium, is a short distance from the River Nene. Posters of previous stars include Noel Cantwell.

Both teams were mid table but Peterborough (website *www. theposh.com*) won fairly easily. Two goals from striker Jonson Clarke-Harris, who has one cap for Jamaica, set them on their way and he was only denied a hat-trick by a smart save just before half time. He also hit the post with a spectacular long range effort before Peterborough added a third 17 minutes from time.

'You're just a shit Stoke City' taunted the supporters.

Peterborough United 3 (Clarke-Harris 26, 36, Ward 73)
Port Vale 0
Attendance 6,138

17. Plymouth Argyll v Ipswich Town

25 September 202 – Home Park – League One

A Sunday 2pm kick-off made a day trip by train to Plymouth feasible, albeit with an early start. But when I got to Reading Station, the departures board said that my 0800 train was delayed leaving Paddington. Luckily the delay was only about 20 minutes and, after a scenic half hour walk up the hill, I entered Home Park, which has a delightful setting, a few minutes before kick-off. Though not before they had sold out of programmes.

This was an important match, with Ipswich top of League One and unbeaten after nine, against Plymouth in fourth place. Early proceedings were fairly even until around then half hour striker Freddie Ladapo, a former Argyll favourite, scored with the aid of a deflection which caused the ball to loop over the goalkeeper. Plymouth were stronger after the break and defender Bali Mumba, on loan from Norwich, shot home from 20 yards. A few minutes later Ipswich dallied in defence and Morgan Whittaker, another loan player, put Plymouth in front from a similar distance.

This gave rise to a frantic final few minutes, culminating in an Ipswich corner deep into stoppage time. They sent keeper Walton up and he got his head to the ball but, agonisingly for Ipswich, it hit the crossbar. The best match I had watched to date.

As a result Plymouth leapfrogged above Ipswich to top the table. I never saw them again that season, but they finished as

League One champions, three points above Ipswich, and the Pilgrims' distinctive green strip will be seen in the championship next season.

I had time before my train back to walk down to Plymouth Hoe and all the statues depicting its proud history. Sadly the walk down Armada Way is now different as the Council decided to fell over 100 trees.

Plymouth Argyll 2 (Mumba 69, Whittaker 75)
Ipswich Town 1 (Lapado 29)
Attendance 15,480

Before the next match I took a two week holiday in the USA. I was able to enjoy New England in the fall, travelling from Boston up to Vermont and Maine. This had the added bonus of missing a good proportion of Liz Truss's premiership.

One amusing incident. I paid a visit to the small town of Clinton Massachusetts, where my great great grandfather had emigrated from Glasgow for a few years in the 1850s to work in the textile mills.

After visiting the Historical society and having a look round, I put the address of the Days Inn I'd booked into the satnav of my hire car and was startled to be told it was over 650 miles away. Muddling up my state abbreviations, I'd booked a room in Clinton, Missouri!

18. Brentford v Brighton & Hove Albion

14 October 2020 – GTech Community Stadium – Premier League

Before this match I had time to go to Wembley for a European Nations League match against Germany. England had a dreadful first half, went 2-0 down, then recovered to go ahead 3-2 before a handling error by Pope handed Germany a late equaliser.

As I explained earlier, my children and I spent many happy hours over the previous 30 years at Griffin Park, which famously had a pub at each of its four corners. In those days Brentford oscillated between the third and fourth tiers, but recently got into the Championship and in 2020, won promotion to the Premier League through the playoffs. At the same time they finally achieved their ambition to move to a larger stadium in 2021, now branded the GTech Community Stadium. It's a remarkably ingenious design feat to fit such a big ground into what was essentially a patch of spare land near Kew Bridge, between the District Line and the A4. It's an intimate stadium with a good viewing experience.

Under Danish manager Thomas Frank they've become a well drilled side, and got a well-deserved win over Brighton, even though the away team had over 70% possession. Bryan Mbeumo hit the bar after 24 minutes, and soon afterwards Ivan Toney gave them the lead with a clever back heel after Frank Onyeka had won a free kick.

I'm a huge fan of Toney, especially his amazing penalty technique, and I was able to observe this from close range after he was brought down just after an hour by Veltman. He simply takes a one step run-up, with his eyes firmly on the goalkeeper, and side foots the ball into the corner. This made it 2-0, and Brentford closed the game out fairly comfortably. Their anthem 'Hey Jude' rang out round the stadium and I repaired to the Greyhound on Kew Green to meet some friends and let the bus queue die down.

Brentford 2 (Toney 27, 64 p) Brighton & HA 0

Attendance 17, 016

19. Gillingham v Stevenage FC

15 October 2022 – MEMS Priestfield Stadium – League Two

I'd been to Priestfield once before, during Manchester City's brief sojourn in the third tier in 1998/9. City won that day but famously, at the end of the season the two teams met again in the playoff final at Wembley – a match which has a massive place in Manchester City folklore. With tickets going for £300 and those only in the Gillingham end, I watched with three City fans in a pub in Wembley.

Gillingham, managed by Tony Pulis, scored twice late on, but City came back from 2-0 down after 85 minutes to level the match and win on penalties to climb out of the third tier at the first attempt. It was probably the most pivotal day in the club's history.

Their ground, Priestfield Stadium has been redeveloped since its original construction in 1893, but has a tired appearance and the visiting supporter's experience isn't enhanced by poor signage and gormless stewarding. Apparently a new stadium is planned.

The game matched 20th v 1st in League Two. Gillingham missed a golden chance, shooting over the bar from about three yards, before Stevenage took the lead with a well-placed header by Danny Rose to the bottom left corner. Gillingham equalised shortly before half time with another well placed header, this time to the other corner. The scorer was Elkan Baggott, who was born in Bangkok and is an international for Indonesia, his mother's country. The second half was uneventful apart from a couple of good saves at either end, and the match ended 1-1.

I didn't see either team again. Gillingham finished 17th, while Stevenage gained automatic promotion to League One with a week of the season to spare.

Gillingham 1 (Baggott 40) Stevenage 1 (Rose 28)
Attendance 5,031

20. Hull City v Birmingham City

16 October 2022 – MKM Stadium – EFL Championship

Another longish train journey for a Sunday afternoon kick-off. The Hull Trains route goes via Doncaster then wanders through East Yorkshire. We passed Selby, with its Drax power station belching smoke into the atmosphere (and apparently providing 6% of our electricity), and the impressive Barton Bridge before arriving at Hull.

Replacing the Old Boothferry Park, the rather nondescript MSM Stadium is about a 20 minute walk from the station. I arrived to an announcement that the kick-off was delayed for 20 minutes because the crossbars were too high! The posts had already been sawn down to correct the error but the delay was to recalibrate the goalline technology system. How many matches had been played before with the goal too high I wondered?

Hull made a bright start with Docherty hitting the side netting early on, but they then conceded a silly penalty for an unnecessary push in the penalty area at a corner. Troy Deeney converted, thumping the ball into the roof of the net. Hull tested the veteran keeper John Ruddy a couple of times, but Birmingham increased their lead shortly after half time, with a spectacular 25 yard left footed shot from Dutch born Curacao international Juninho Bacuna. They should have made it 3-0 when their striker was cleaned out by the Hull goalkeeper when through on goal. But this time Deeney's powerful penalty sailed over the bar. The result put Birmingham into the top half, and left Hull only one point above the drop zone.

Before catching my train back, I had time visit the Clarendon Arms to watch the Liverpool beat Manchester City 1-0. It was my first visit to Hull, and I didn't see anything to make me want to return.

Hull City 0 Birmingham City 2 (Deeney 14 p, Bacuna 47)
Attendance 16,587

21. Norwich City v Luton Town

18 Ocotber 2022 – Carrow Road – EFL Championship

I'd hardly spent any time in Norwich before, and the evening kick-off gave me the chance for some tourism. The Castle was closed for renovation, but there was plenty else to see – a couple of good museums, including Bridewell Prison, the Cathedral, a statue to commemorate Edith Cavell, and Cow Tower, a 14th century artillery tower.

When the Carrow Road Stadium was redeveloped in 2002, it will have been in quite a rural setting just across the River Wensum, but the area has been extensively developed with some trendy housing. I was able to fuel up at £1.69 a pint in the local Wetherspoons, with the splendid name 'The Queen of Iceni'.

Both clubs were pushing for promotion but my concentration on the match was less than total. My local club, Hampton and Richmond Borough, were playing a FA Cup replay against Torquay United for a place in the first round proper, so I had the commentary feed in my headphones. (Hampton lost!) Teemu Pukki carved out a couple of chances for Norwich but the only goal of the match was well taken in the 62nd minute by Luton striker Carlton Morris, who was playing for his ninth club, after Norwich had lost possession on halfway. Norwich's cause was made harder a few minutes later when their Scottish international Kenny McLean was given a straight red card for use of an elbow at a corner.

As a result Luton jumped one place above Norwich into 4th place. I never watched Norwich again; they fell away to finish 13th.

Norwich City 0 Luton Town 1 (Morris 62)
Attendance 25,846

22. AFC Bournemouth v Southampton

19 October 2022 – Vitality Stadium – Premier League

I watched this match courtesy of my good friend John, a retired air traffic controller and lifelong Cherries supporter. John kindly let me use his sister's season ticket as she was on holiday, and also did the driving – a big help as he knows the short cuts.

Dean Court, currently trading as the Vitality Stadium, was originally built in 1910 for Boscombe FC. It was rebuilt in 2002 but remained the smallest and most basic ground in the Premier League.

Bournemouth entered the game on the back of a six match unbeaten run under Gary O'Neill, who had been installed as caretaker manager after the departure of Scott Parker. Southampton on the other hand were deep in relegation mire. They had spent in the summer, but my Saints supporting friends said their weakness was the lack of a striker.

Notwithstanding that, they took an early lead when some slack marking allowed Che Adams to head home from close range. After that Ward Prowse exercised his usual control in midfield. The end of the first half was livened up by a spat between Mepham and Maitland-Niles. Bournemouth pressed more in the second half and went close through Solanki, but they couldn't break down the Southampton defence, though they had a strong shout for a penalty right at the end. This win was a reprieve for their beleaguered manager Ralph Hassenhutl, though it proved to be only temporary. Bournemouth, having looked in big trouble for a time, went on to finish 15th, though strangely this was not enough to keep O'Neill his job.

The return journey was uneventful apart from an ominous flash from a speed camera.

Bournemouth 0 Southampton 1 (Adams 9)
Attendance 10,405

23. Fulham v Aston Villa

20 October 2022 – Craven Cottage – Premier League

I've always had a soft spot for Fulham, and Craven Cottage is one of my favourite grounds. When I first went there was no Riverside stand so, on the appropriate day, spectators had a free view of the Boat Race. I have a vivid memory of going to a 4th round cup match against West Bromwich in 1969. David Coleman was doing the Match of the Day commentary from an open hut at the back of the Putney Road end, and in quieter moments we could hear his commentary, which sometimes provoked ribald mimicking. At half time he cheerfully responded to request from spectators for updates from other matches – no transistor radios then!

Fulham had made a bright start to the season, having come top of the Championship in 2021/2 to clinch promotion. Villa were in less good shape. The Brazilian Willian – an inspired close season signing – immediately caught my eye, still very lively at the age of 34, and he soon brought a smart save from Martinez. After 34 minutes Fulham went ahead. Martinez punched a corner clear to Harrison Reed, who returned it with interest. Villa made life harder for themselves when Douglas Luiz collected a red card. He leaned his head towards Mitrovic, who collapsed to the floor as if he'd been hit by Tyson Fury. Mitrovic then doubled the lead from the penalty spot after Matty Cash handled, and a Tyrone Mings own goal made it 3-0.

A comfortable win took Fulham into the top half of the table, while only goal difference kept Villa out of the drop zone.

'You're getting sacked in the morning' crowed the Fulham fans to Steven Gerrard, but their timescale proved conservative. He'd gone by the time I got home. Villa made an inspired selection to replace him with Unai Emery, who took them from 17th to 7th in the table, and a place in Europe.

Fulham 3 (Reed 36, Mitrovic 68p, Mings og 83) Aston Villa 0
Attendance 23,508

24. Sutton United v Walsall

22 October 2020 – Gander Lane – League Two

Next up was a local trip to Sutton united for a League Two match against Walsall. Sutton had a proud history as a non-league club, with a famous FA Cup win against Coventry in 1989, and a run to the 5th round in 2017, beating three Football League teams before losing to Arsenal. They had installed an artificial pitch at their Gander Lane ground, but had to revert to turf when they finally achieved Football League status in 2021. It still feels a bit like a non-league ground though, with a giraffe as a mascot as an odd touch.

Playing in yellow, Sutton had an early present when Walsall's Brandon Comley – a Montserrat international – contrived to pick up two yellow cards within ten minutes for fouls on the same player. But they didn't make the advantage count until well into the second half, when a clumsy challenge gave away a penalty converted by veteran Rob Milsom. Walsall responded with a triple substitution. Sutton almost extended their lead when Randall had a fierce 25 yard shot tipped over, but Walsall rescued a point when substitute Maddox scored with a low shot four minutes from time.

The result left the two teams in 14th and 15th place, and they both ended the season in similar positions.

Sutton United 1 (Millsom 72p) Walsall 1 (Maddox 86)
Attendance 2,773

25. Sheffield Wednesday v Bristol Rovers

22 October 2022 – Hillsborough – League Two

When I checked into my hotel for this midweek match the receptionist leaned forward conspiratorially and said 'one of the teams is staying here tonight.' 'Let me guess', I said 'it's probably the away team'. She seemed suitably impressed by my powers of logical deduction.

Hillsborough is of course forever associated with the 1989 tragedy, and I was a little surprised when the tram stop for the stadium was Leppings Lane. I would have thought that, like Rillington Place, it might have benefitted from a rebrand. The 19th century stadium has a certain faded grandeur, and the Leppings Lane tunnel was again subject of criticism at a subsequent FA Cup tie against Newcastle, which resulted in a capacity reduction being imposed.

Darren Moore's team were challenging for promotion and made the early running, with Josh Windass prominent. Then a couple of pieces of defensive carelessness presented Bristol Rovers with chances, which drew smart saves from Stockdale. Wednesday finally got their reward in first half stoppage time, when striker Michael Smith glanced home an unstoppable header. Then from nowhere, the visitors levelled on the hour, when Josh Coburn, on loan from Middlesbrough, clipped a through ball neatly over Stockdale and into the far corner.

I'd hoped I might bump into Bristol Rovers manager Joey

Barton over breakfast the next morning but they had left early. The space their coach had occupied now contained the bus of the Greece Rugby League team, who were competing in the World Cup. It's not a sport I associate with Greece, and they were duly beaten 96-4 by England on the Saturday. Before catching my train home I had time to visit the National Emergency Services Museum, which is very child friendly and has a splendid collection of old fire engines and ambulances.

Sheffield Wednesday 1 (Smith 45+3) Bristol Rovers 1 (Coburn 60) Attendance 22,006

26. Manchester United v FC Sheriff Tiraspol

27 October 2022 – Old Trafford – Europa Cup

I used to go to Old Trafford a lot in my youth. My most memorable match was a 2-0 win against the great 1961 Spurs team which won the double. United keeper Harry Gregg, having got injured, hobbled on the wing (no subs then of course) and set up the second United goal. I've looked up the teams for that day and they included Cantwell, Foulkes, Setters, Quixall and Charlton for United, Blanchflower, Norman, Mackay, Allen, Smith and White for Spurs. Stadium capacity then was 62,000 but the gate that day was over 65,000 – a scary and quite dangerous crush. My most recent match at Old Trafford was when Beckham scored his memorable injury time free kick to draw with Greece and take England to the 2002 World Cup finals.

As I walked from the cricket ground down Sir Matt Busby way there was no demand for the Ronaldo scarves which the vendors were keen to offload. The stadium now holds over 74,000 and was almost full when I took my seat in the Stretford end where, amazingly, they were selling Madri at £3 a pint. Opponents for this Europa Cup group were Sheriff Tiraspol, from the small unrecognised Russian enclave of Transnistria in Moldova. Owned by a wealthy supermarket billionaire they had bought repeated success in the Moldova League, and achieved fame the previous season by beating Real Madrid at the Bernabeu.

The match was predictably one sided. Bruno Fernandes bossed the midfield – what a pity his undoubted talent is spoilt by his unpleasant, whingeing personality. I was particularly impressed by a young Argentinian winger who I hadn't seen before, Alejandro Garnacho, who was born a few days after Ronaldo helped Portugal eliminate England at Euro 2004. We were to see plenty more of him before the season ended. Sheriff held out almost till half time when Dalot headed in from a corner. Rashford added a second and then shortly before the end, Ronaldo scored. His first header was saved, but he followed up alertly and poked the ball home. It was his 104th goal for the club and it turned out to be his last as, within a couple of weeks, United released him from his contract and he headed off to the flesh pots of Saudi Arabia to earn a few more squillion. Bad news for the scarf vendors.

**Manchester United 3 (Dalot 44, Rashford 65,
Ronaldo 81) FC Sheriff 0
Attendance 73,764**

27. Cheltenham Town v Milton Keynes Dons

29 October 2022 – Completely-Suzuki Stadium
– League One

My father died in Cheltenham and my parents ashes are interred in the local church, so I took some flowers and cleaned up the little memorial stone. It has always upset me that the adjacent stone commemorates two twin girls, Emma and Becky, who were not only born on the same day but died on the same day, aged 18. I always assumed it was a car crash, but on this occasion my curiosity led me to Google, where I discovered the more gruesome truth. They were tragically burned to death in a barn fire.

Before the Cheltenham match I watched Manchester City at Leicester in the lunchtime kick-off. They struggled to break down Leicester's defence until De Bruyne scored with a trademark free kick. Then I walked to the ground which has had various commercial names, including the World of Smile Stadium, and was now the Completely-Suzuki Stadium. Is there a Partial-Suzuki Stadium nearby, I wonder? One of its stands was named the HGV Drivers Stand and the ground has a nice outdoor bar called the Thirsty Robins where many spectators were enjoying a pre-match pint in the autumn sun.

The match against MK Dons produced my first 0-0 draw, though it wasn't as dull as the scoreline suggests. MK Dons had slightly the better of the play, and were only denied victory by an athletic save in the last minute by the Cheltenham goalkeeper. Dons 38 year-old full back Dean Lewington (son of former England assistant manager Ray) had played for the club since 2004 and, in the last match of the season, played his 765th match for the club, overtaking Jimmy Dickinson's record 764 appearances for Portsmouth.

Both teams ended the day where they started – too close to relegation for comfort.

Cheltenham Town 0 MK Dons 0
Attendance 3,365

28. Wycombe Wanderers v Port Vale

1 November 2022 – Adams Stadium – League One

I'd been to Adams Park once, in 1998/9 during Manchester City's one season in the third tier, then called Division Two. Travelling after work, I was stuck in horrible traffic and only got into the ground after 20 minutes, just in time to see Wycombe score the only goal of the match. That defeat was the nadir of my 70 years watching City.

Adams Park, to the west of High Wycombe, has a capacity of over 10,000 and was home to Wasps rugby club for 12 seasons. It was less than half full for this midweek game. Not having eaten beforehand, I bought a pie which not only cost £7, but was truly disgusting.

Both teams were just above halfway in the table. Wycombe took the lead early on with a fierce left-footed shot from outside the area from the London born Albanian Mehmeti. They held the lead until the 52nd minute (!) of the first half, when Port Vale equalised following a corner. Another long range shot put Wycombe in front but, 13 minutes from time, they conceded an unnecessary corner and Port Vale equalised through Bob Conlon, whose great grandfather had apparently kept goal for Port Vale from 1937 to 1952.

It was to be the only time I watched Wycombe, who eventually finished in a respectable 9th place.

Wycombe Wanderers 2 (Mehmeti 4, Wing 61) Port Vale 2 (Wilson 45+7, Conlon 77)

Attendance 4,192

29. Arsenal v FC Zurich

3 November 2022 – Emirates Stadium – Europa
League

I had the pleasure of going to this match with my son Adam, who has been a devoted Arsenal supporter since he first followed football, having fallen in love with them when they had a great squad which included the wonderful Thierry Henri.

This was the last round of group matches in the Europa League and Arsenal needed to win to come top, to avoid an extra round. They were still top of the Premier League, a position they had held since the end of August to the surprise of many. Their squad had been much strengthened by the signing of Jesus and Zinchenko from Manchester City. Zurich FC were bottom of the Swiss Premier League.

As is usually the case with European matches, the away support added to the atmosphere, and at kick-off the ground was covered with a blue haze from smoke bombs. Zinchenko, returning from injury, was on the bench that night and it was his replacement, Kieran Tierney, who put Arsenal in front with a high quality strike from 20 yards, after Ben White's shot had been blocked at the end of an excellent move. Arsenal looked the stronger team, and enjoyed over 60% possession without increasing their lead, though Jesus was conspicuously active and Nketiah had a good header saved. Inevitably, Zurich applied some pressure towards the end, so there were a nervous final few minutes, but Arsenal held on for the win.

Coming top of their group meant they didn't have to play in the round of 32 but that didn't do them any good as they went out on penalties in the round of 16 to Sporting Lisbon.

Arsenal 1 (Tierney 17) FC Zurich 0
Attendance 48,500

30. Reading v Preston North End

4 November 22 – Select Car Leasing Stadium – League One

The Majewski Stadium boringly now trades as the Select Car Leasing Stadium, and it took me ages to get in as the signage for car parking is atrocious.

Preston had promotion ambitions, while Reading were mid table. They had a father and son combination on display, being managed by Paul Ince with his son Tom in midfield. They also featured a golden oldie in Andy Carroll, who I'd last seen playing for England in Kiev when we were knocked out on penalties by Italy in Euro 2012. It is a measure of how little teams played the ball out from the back then, that England's most used passing combination that evening was Joe Hart to Carroll.

Carroll announced himself with a wild volley into row Z, and Preston's Irish international Robbie Brady brought a smart save from the Reading keeper, but the match was 0-0 at half time. Shortly after half time, Brady then provided an assist for the opening goal, delivering a free kick onto the head of Ched Evans – his first goal in 35 matches apparently. Brady was then involved in levelling the match up by conceding a penalty, which was converted by Angola international Joao. Finally Evans celebrated the end of his goal drought by scoring the winner for Preston with a fierce cross shot 11 minutes from time.

A novel feature of the half time entertainment was that, instead of the usual penalty shoot-outs etc, the sponsors held a raffle and drew at random a row of seats which would be eligible for a free slice of pizza. It was their lucky evening, as the row of seats drawn was unoccupied.

**Reading 1 (Joao 71p) Preston North End 2 (Evans 51, 79)
Attendance 11,777**

31. Nottingham Forest v Brentford

5 November 2022 – The City Ground – Premier League

I'd been to nearby Trent Bridge cricket ground many times, but this was my first visit to the City Ground. My visit had an interesting start when the attendant at the nearby municipal car park cheerfully took my £5, without telling me that the facility was already full. Several other cars were in the same boat, and some creative parking was called for.

The stadium on the banks of the River Trent has been home to Nottingham Forest since 1898. My seat was in the away end, as I'm a member at Brentford. There was some action even before the start – a physical altercation between one of the ground staff and the Brentford goalkeeping coach! A dispute about the unauthorised use of the penalty area apparently. Four months later, the FA got round to charging them with improper conduct and they were both given a fine and a ban.

Forest had just regained Premier League status after an absence of over 20 years. They had two speedy forwards in Morgan Gibbs-White and Brennan Johnson, and the former gave them the lead after 20 minutes with a shot which deflected in off Ben Mee – his first goal since joining from Wolves for £42 million. At the far end, just before half time, Mbeumo played Wissa in on goal. Wissa rounded Henderson and then went down. A Brentford supporter next to me reckoned he'd tripped over his own feet, but there was a long VAR review which ended with Andre Marriner being sent to the monitor, hotly pursued by Henderson protesting that he'd touched the ball. As is almost always the case when the monitor is consulted, Marriner changed his mind, awarded the penalty and booked Henderson. The goalkeeper carried on moaning and it would have served him right if he'd got a second yellow card. With 15 minutes to go, Wissa seemed to have won the match for Brentford with a skilful lob, but right at the death Gibbs-White's shot struck Jorgensen and just crossed the line. It took goalline technology to award the goal which then survived a VAR check for offside, again with spectators kept in the dark.

An entertaining match and a fair result.

Rather than drive all the way home, I stayed overnight at Huntingdon, and spent a pleasant Sunday morning doing a rural walk in the pretty town of Godmanchester.

Nottingham Forest 2 (Gibbs-White 20, Jorgensen og 90)
Brentford 2 (Mbeumo 45+3(p), Wissa 75)
Attendance 28,869

32. Leicester City v Newport County

8 November 2022 – King Power Stadium –
Round 3 Carabao Cup

Next up I had a couple of Carabao Cup matches.

Shortly after I joined BOAC (the predecessor of British Airways) in the late 1960s, I worked in the same office as a nice young guy on the graduate trainee scheme called Tim Stevens. Tim didn't stay long at the company, but left to pursue his vocation and join the church. Bring a capable chap he soon climbed the Church of England's corporate ladder, as I'm sure he would have done had he stayed in the airline, and eventually became Bishop of Leicester. As a result, in 2013 he briefly became a national figure on our television screens when he conducted the funeral service for Richard III. On arrival at Leicester I was able to visit Richard's tomb, and enjoy the splendid visitor centre which tells the remarkable story of the discovery of his remains under a municipal carpark.

I'd been to Leicester City's old Filbert Street ground in 1959. Manchester City scored first and lost 8-4! You don't get scores like that anymore.

As I walked to the King Power Stadium I came across the only suggestion of violence I encountered in my 92 matches. A gaggle of weedy looking Newport supporters were trying to square up to some home fans. The police soon sent them on their way, and they marched to the ground proudly singing the standard anthem of Welsh fans – 'we know who we are, we know who we are, we're only sheep shaggers, that's who we are.' The stadium was less than half full, and the away fans were put in one corner at least 50 yards from anyone else.

Three years earlier Newport had caused a major upset by dumping Leicester out of the FA Cup. There was no suggestion of a repeat this time, though it took Leicester almost till half time to score – a curling left foot shot from James Justin which went in off then post. Sadly for the defender, who some thought would be on Southgate's short list for Qatar, he was carried off on a stretcher after about an hour. The second half gave me the chance to witness a couple of fine goals by Jamie Vardy in the twilight of his career. The first was a quality glancing header from Albrighton's cross, and for the second he rounded the goalkeeper and sat him down before slamming the ball into the empty net.

Leicester City 3 (Justin 44, Vardy 70, 82) Newport County 0
Attendance 15,081

33. Liverpool v Derby County

9 November 2022 – Anfield – Round 3 Carabao
Cup

Industrial (in)action by Mick Flynn and his RMT members
meant that I had to use National Express to travel from Leicester
to Liverpool. This was relatively painless, involving a change
at Birmingham. The bus station is located next to a huge hole
in the ground. In several years and after a few billion pounds,
this will be the site of Birmingham's HS2 station, though the
government subsequently downgraded this nonsense vanity
project by cancelling the northern extension, so that the line will
one day effectively be a shuttle between Acton and Aston.

I was at Anfield for the 2018 Champions League match
when Liverpool battered Manchester City 3-0, after City's coach
had been attacked by spectators en route to the ground. The
atmosphere that night was awesomely intimidating.

Tonight's match was much more low key. Liverpool played
virtually a reserve team with an average age just over 22. Only
Gomez and Oxlade Chamberlain were present from their regular
squad, though Firminho, Elliot and Darwin Nunes came on
after just over an hour. They were followed onto the pitch by Ben
Doak, on the eve of his 17th birthday. Despite the strength of the
opposition, Derby thwarted Liverpool for 90 minutes. Mercifully
we were spared extra time and went straight to penalties, which
took place in front of 5,600 very vocal Derby fans. The shootout
soon turned in Liverpool's favour as, although Bajetic missed
first for Liverpool, Alisson's understudy, Irish international

Caoimhin Kelleher, saved three of the five Derby kicks he faced. An undistinguished shootout, which afforded some amusement when Firminho, attempting a Panenka, chipped the ball gently into the stand.

Liverpool 0 Derby County 0
(Liverpool won 3-2 on penalties)
Attendance 52,608

34. Newport County v Stockport County

12 November 2022 – Rodney Parade – League Two

The principle about the frequency of buses applied here. I'd lived my whole life without ever watching Newport County, and now I saw them twice in 5 days. The train takes only just over an hour from Reading, so I was able to arrive in time to watch Manchester City v Brentford in the lunchtime kick-off. Two goals from Ivan Toney – the last in the 98th minute – delivered an unexpected and unwelcome defeat to City in the last match before the World Cup break.

The walk to the ground goes past the fairly ruined 14th century castle, then across the River Usk to Rodney Parade. This quaint ground is the second oldest in the Football League, having opened in 1879, and installed floodlights only two years later. It is a dual use ground, being also the home of Welsh regional team Dragons RFC.

The visitors were Stockport County, whose 500 supporters made a bad start by chanting through the Armistice Day minute's silence, though I think the PA contributed to this by not making a clear announcement. Stockport hadn't conceded a goal in their previous six games, but went behind on the stroke of half time when fullback Aaron Lewis bundled the ball home at the far post. Newport equalised in the 54th minute when the Stockport goalkeeper made a hash of a free kick from the right.

There then followed a strange incident. A Stockport defender, thinking the whistle had gone, picked the ball up on the edge of the area, whereupon Newport players howled for a free kick/red card. The ref consulted his linesman, who confirmed he'd heard a whistle and, with a commendable application of common sense, play was restarted with a dropped ball. Irish striker Paddy Madden scored the winner for Stockport a quarter of an hour from time, bundling the ball home at the far post.

It was Newport's first defeat under their new manager Graham Coughlan. It left them in 19th place but they had a respectable second half to their season and finished 15th.

Newport County 1 (Lewis 45) Stockport County 2
(Hussey 54, Madden 74)
Attendance 3,754

35. Hartlepool United v Solihull Moors

15 November 2022 – Suit Direct Stadium (Victoria Park) – FA Cup Round 1 Replay

Next I went up north for two FA Cup first round replays. The first was at Hartlepool's Victoria Park after National League team Solihull Moors had twice come from behind to force a 2-2 draw in the first leg.

The-136-year-old Victoria Park ground had the unusual distinction of being bombed by a German zeppelin in 1916. It has recently, like many other stadiums, accepted corporate sponsorship, and now carries another silly name – the Suit Direct Stadium. The ground has a stand named after Cyril Knowles, who was managing them in 1990/91, the season they gained promotion from Division 4, but tragically had to give up mid-season after being diagnosed with a brain tumour, from which he died later that year.

Hartlepool, after starting their season with 9 matches without a win, had appointed Keith Curle, who played five seasons at Manchester City, as their manager. Within 8 minutes they found themselves a goal behind, when Solihull's Ryan Barnett scored with a cross shot from the right following a corner. They looked like going out of the tournament until they equalised in the 90th minute. The scorer was Reghan Tumilty, who had moved south from Raith Rovers because he said he was 'fed up with playing against the same nine teams over and over again'. Extra time was scoreless, with Solihull shooting wide a couple of times.

66

Solihull got off to the worst possible start in the shootout when their kicker slipped and shot miles over the bar, John Terry style. Their second was easily saved, and Hartlepool ran out winners 4-3.

Though they made it to the 3rd round of the FA Cup before losing to Stoke, the rest of the season didn't go well for Hartlepool. Keith Curle left in January, and they finished in 23rd place, so the club of Brian Clough and Jeff Stelling was relegated to the National League.

Hartlepool ranks pretty low down my list of desirable destinations but, despite its status as a fairly rundown and deprived town, it has a hidden treasure, the National Museum of the Royal Navy. This contains the spectacular HMS Trincomalee, built in Bombay in 1817, the oldest British warship still afloat. It had seen service in the West Indies and Canada performing, among other things, anti-slavery patrols in the West Indies. I spent a happy couple of hours there learning about life on 19th century warships, before catching a train to York and Manchester.

Hartlepool Rovers 1 (Tumilty 90) Solihull Moors 1 (Barnett 8)
(Extra time, Hartlepool won 3-2 on penalties)
Attendance 2,170

36. Salford City v Peterborough United

16 November 2022 – Peninsula Stadium – FA Cup Round 1 Replay

Salford City is best known for the financial involvement of Manchester United's 'Class of 92', the Neville brothers, Paul Scholes and Nicky Butt, who had bought an interest in 2014. Known as the Ammies because of their amateur antecedents, Salford climbed out of the Northern Premier League and then, after turning fully professional, achieved Football League status in 2019.

The Moor Lane ground/Peninsula Stadium is in Kersal, right on the border with Bury, in a strongly Jewish area of Manchester where the kids playing five-a-side were all wearing yarmulkes. Before the stadium was built it was for many years the home of Manchester Rugby Club, where my father played for a bit in the 1930s. The club issued a team sheet with the programme, which was a nice touch, and a tasty sausage and chips cost £3.

League Two Salford had held League One Peterborough to a 0-0 draw in a first leg so devoid of action that YouTube could only spin the highlights out for 58 seconds.

Despite now having home advantage, Salford never looked like pulling off an upset. Ephron Mason-Clark put Peterborough in front with a fierce shot just before half time, and Marriott scored twice in five minutes near the end to wrap the tie up.

'We battered them at Peterborough' I overheard a supporter complaining as I left. If they did, it didn't show in the YouTube clip I watched, or the score.

Salford City 0 Peterborough United 3
(Mason-Clark 39, Marriott 78, 83)
Attendance 1,059

37. Portsmouth v Derby County

18 November 2022 – Fratton Park – League One

A Friday evening fixture at Fratton Park gave me the chance to spend the whole day at the Historic Royal Navy Dockyard. I saw the Mary Rose, which I hadn't seen since it had been given its splendid new home, HMS Victory, and a wonderful ship called M33. The new Mary Rose display setting is brilliant, showing many aspects of its brief life. The M33 is the only surviving Royal Navy ship from the Gallipoli campaign. It was ordered in March 1915, launched in May and commissioned in June. They didn't hang around in those days.

Fratton Park was opened in 1899 and has been Portsmouth's ground ever since. Apparently it was given that name to convince spectators that it was near Fratton railway station, though it is actually almost a mile away. Portsmouth and Derby were both in the play-off places, and they fought a goalless draw which left them 5th and 6th respectively, separated only by a single goal in goal difference. Derby made a lot of the running, and David McGoldrick hit the bar early on. But neither side scored, with Portsmouth not registering a shot on target until stoppage time.

I stayed overnight in Portsmouth and, before driving to my next match in Swindon, spent some time at Porchester Castle – a well preserved Norman fort which has also been used as a prison, notably holding over 7,000 French prisoners during the Napoleonic Wars.

Climbing the tower affords a magnificent view of Portsmouth Harbour and the Solent.

Portsmouth 0 Derby County 0
Attendance 18,623

38. Swindon Town v Crewe Alexandra

19 November 2022 – The County Ground – League Two

My long standing friend Roger is a lifelong Swindon supporter and, one cold November evening in 1979, we set off down the M4 to the County Ground to watch Swindon play a League Cup quarter final against Arsenal, who they had famously beaten in the final at Wembley 10 years earlier. Swindon threatened another upset by scoring twice in the first 15 minutes. It was before fans were segregated and we had a particularly loud mouthed Arsenal fan in front of us, who had clearly won his fight against anorexia. When the second goal went in he bet Roger £5, which would have bought a good dinner back then, on the result. Arsenal then scored, Swindon got another, but Arsenal hit back with two more to level the match at 3-3 after 90 minutes. The first division side would have been expected to go on and win from there but Swindon scored next and, amid great excitement, held on for a famous 4-3 win.. Roger, perhaps naively, held out his hand for his £5, but matey simply swore fluently at him and waddled off.

The County ground hadn't changed a lot in the intervening 43 years. They sell pasties, not pies, presumably trying to burnish their West Country credentials. And I was struck by a sign saying that adults trying to enter the ground with reduced rate tickets would have their tickets confiscated with no refund given. Are Swindonians more fraudulent than average?

The opponents were Crewe Alexandra. The match couldn't match the 1979 Arsenal match for excitement, and the only goal came from a penalty, awarded to Crewe after 23 minutes for a foul just on the edge of the area. It was converted, Ivan Toney style, by Dan Agyei who thumped the ball into the roof of the net. Swindon had several close efforts, including one from Jephcott, on loan from Plymouth, which hit the bar, but they couldn't score, and their run of five matches unbeaten came to an end. They went on to have a standard mid-table season, finishing 10th in League Two.

Swindon Town 0 Crewe Alexandra 1 (Agyei 23 pen)
Attendance 8,734

39. Forest Green Rovers v Alvechurch FC

26 November 2022 – Innocent New Lawn Stadium – FA Cup Round 2

The last weekend in November saw the second round of the FA Cup, and I went to two matches involving non-league opposition.

The operative word in the name of Forest Green Rovers is 'green'. Their owner Dale Vince is an industrialist and deeply committed environmentalist. He spent his early adult life as a new age traveller, and his dress sense raises eyebrows when he's being entertained to lunch in visiting board rooms. He founded, and had recently sold, the green energy company Ecotricity. He had recently courted controversy by giving money not only to the Labour Party, but also to the Stop Oil movement, acts which had predictably caused the Daily Mail and Daily Express to foam at the mouth, to mix a metaphor.

Forest Green Rovers is tucked away in the Cotswolds, near Nailsworth. Its small ground, the Innocent New Lawn Stadium, is a monument to sustainability. It has the world's first organic football pitch, which is cut automatically by a solar powered mower called the Mowbot which is guided by GPS technology. In a gesture calculated to further enrage the Mail and Express, the flag of Palestine was flown.

My friend Danny had kindly arranged VIP match tickets which included hospitality, the lunch of course being vegan. FGR's opponents were Alvechurch FC, who play in the seventh tier Southern League Premier Division, and had upset League One Cheltenham to earn this match. Alvechurch is just up the road in Worcestershire, so they were able to bring lots of supporters; perhaps half of the crowd were away fans. We sat with some of them at lunch who were friends of Josh March, who had progressed from Alvechurch to play for FGR.

The home team, who play in organic kit, took the lead after 4 minutes when the aforementioned March won a soft penalty. Alvechurch equalised just after half time through a stunning free kick from Jed Abbey, a former Wolves junior. But their lead only lasted a couple of minutes. Alvechurch failed to clear a cross from the left, and March bundled the ball into the goal. The last 18 minutes was made more interesting when FGR's Bernard picked up a second yellow card, but they held on to progress to the third round, in which they were knocked out by Birmingham City.

Forest Green Rovers 2 (Wickham 24 pen, March 51)
Alvechurch 1 (Abbey 49)
Attendance 2,758

40. Bristol Rovers v Borehamwood FC

27 November 2022 – Memorial Stadium – FA Cup Round 2

My second trip to the West Country in 24 hours was for a Sunday afternoon match at Bristol Rovers., They are known locally as 'The Gas' because their previous home at Eastville was next to a gasworks, which presumably contributed to the atmosphere! They now play at the Memorial Stadium, built in 1996, which has a lovely view over the city. It was easy to find on street parking close by.

Their opponents were Borehamwood from the National League, who had had a club record cup run the previous season, beating AFC Wimbledon and Bournemouth to reach the 5th found, before losing a high profile match at Everton, then managed by Carlo Ancelotti.

Bristol Rovers had experienced a lot of sickness in the club, forcing Joey Barton to field a much weakened team. Bristol nearly scored with an overhead kick before Borehamwood took the lead with a neat goal, developed on the training ground. A corner on the right was pulled back to the edge of the 'D', where unmarked Broadbent's shot went in via a deflection off defender Evans. Borehamwood then hit a post and had a goal ruled out for offside, before doubling their lead with a looping header from their other central defender David Stephens. Bristol Rovers made very little impression on their National League opponents, not having a serious shot until the 82nd minute. The crowd took the defeat with resignation.

Borehamwood advanced to the third round for the third consecutive year, when, after drawing at home against Accrington, they lost 1-0 in the replay.

Bristol Rovers 0 Borehamwood 2 (Broadbent 17, Stephens 29)
Attendance 4,769

41. Leyton Orient v Bradford City

3 December 2022 – Breyer Group Stadium (Brisbane Road) – League Two

When I checked for my ticket a couple of days before this match, I discovered that I hadn't actually bought one! Luckily my senior moment wasn't fatal as the match wasn't quite sold out, and I was able to get a seat, albeit in one corner. I had only been to Leyton Orient once before, in 1980 for a FA Cup replay against Altrincham, my home team from Cheshire, who had Alex Stepney, aged 38, in goal. Their Brisbane Road ground, currently known as the Breyer Group Stadium, dates back to the 19th century. It is easily reached from Leyton Station, and one of its stands was recently named after their former manager Justin Edinburgh, who died from a heart attack in 2019, aged 49. Outside the stadium is a statue commemorating another fine player who died much too young, Laurie Cunningham.

Leyton Orient were the pace setters in League Two, and the previous week the club had given a new contract to their manager Richie Wellens. He belongs to the school of managers who considers a large part of his job is to hassle the fourth official. I always think this is a relatively pointless pastime, done more for the cameras than for any real effect.

Orient took the lead after 24 minutes when Charlie Kelman, on loan from QPR, received an incisive through ball, and was able to round the goalkeeper. Bradford then missed a sitter before Orient doubled their lead with a goal that replicated the one scored at Swindon – a corner cut back to the 'D' and a fine shot, this time not needing a deflection. Bradford threatened very little, and Orient wrapped the match up with a third goal five minutes from time.

This win left them five points clear at the top of League Two, with Bradford sixth.

Leyton Orient 3 (Kelman 24, James 32, Sotiriou 85)
Bradford City 0
Attendance 8,671

42. Stockport County v Charlton Athletic

7 December 2022 – Edgeley Park Stadium – FA Cup Round 2 Replay

This was the worst of the many train journeys involved in my project. And it wasn't down to industrial action. When I got to Euston, the board showed that my train to Manchester was delayed. We then boarded, but were told we'd be held for up to an hour. After about 30 minutes, we were then told that all trains out of Euston were suspended. An 'incident' on the line to Watford – a 'jumper' in the industry jargon. So I took the tube to Kings Cross, and caught the next train to Leeds, standing/sitting in the corridor the whole way. Then a stopping Trans Pennine train to Manchester, before getting to Stockport. I just had time to check-in to my accommodation before walking to Edgeley Park.

After my six hour journey I was gagging for a pint, so wasn't best pleased to discover the ground was alcohol free. I was also hungry and, to make matters worse, made the mistake of ordering a 'meat' pie whose contents were of dubious origin.

Stockport had earned this replay with a 97th minute equaliser to draw at The Valley, and in the intervening 10 days Charlton had sacked their manager. They got a lucky break when the Stockport goalkeeper punched a corner clear, only to see it rebound from his fullback into the net. County levelled in the 25th minute, midfielder Will Collar picking up a rebound from the post.

Sitting on the end of a row means spending the first five minutes of the second half letting people back to their seats, and this caused me to miss the liveliest event of the match. A Charlton player clattered a Stockport player into the advertising hoardings, and all hell broke loose for several minutes. The guy in front said that if he'd done that on the street he'd have been charged with assault. When the dust settled, Collar scored two more, completing his hat-trick from the penalty spot.

Thankfully my journey home was less eventful than the way up. Stockport's giant killing won them a third round match at home to Walsall, which they lost.

Stockport County 3 (Collar 25, 73, 81p)
Charlton Athletic 1 (Wright og 7)
Attendance 6,242

43. Queens Park Rangers v Burnley

11 December 2022 – Loftus Road – EFL Championship

I went to this Sunday afternoon match with my good friend Ray, a lifelong supporter and season ticket holder, and his friend Paolo who had flown in especially from Italy, despite horrible airline delays. The pre-match ritual comprised lunch at Pizza Express. I've always liked Loftus Road, with its tight ground and intimate atmosphere. Ray's seats are within abusing distance of the lino, though the seat pitch is comparable to Ryanair.

Since I'd watched them, Vincent Kompany's Burnley were setting the pace in the Championship, while QPR were in temporary hands, as their manager Michael Beale had left them to manage another Rangers, north of the border.

QPR started with a strong appeal for a penalty which was turned down, then fell behind to a beautifully struck free kick from Iceland international Johann Gudmundsson. Shortly before half time Netherlands under 21 international Ian Maatsen made it 2-0, after the keeper had palmed out Vitinho's shot. QPR brought on two subs at half time, including Albert Adomah, known as 'Uncle Albert' because of his advancing years. Born in North London, Adomah had begun his career at Old Meadonians in Chiswick where my older boys used to play, and actually started in their 7th XI before working his way up to play for Middlesbrough and

Aston Villa, as well as winning 19 caps for Ghana. Sadly he had little influence on the result, and Burnley added a third goal after a defensive error.

'Stand up if you hate Mick Beale' chanted the fans. The result restored Burnley's three point lead. QPR went on a horrendous run which saw them fall from sixth to the bottom three before an unexpected late season win at Stoke eased their relegation worries.

QPR 0 Burnley 3 (Gudmundsson 19, Maatsen 45+3, Tella 71)
Attendance 14,299

44. Birmingham City v Reading

16 December 2022 – St Andrews – EFL
Championship

It was a freezing day and the journey by road took almost three hours. I'd picked a slightly grotty pub on the basis that it was only 20 minutes from the ground. But the walk was downhill and very icy!

St Andrews is over 100 years old, but has been redeveloped into a pleasant modern stadium holding a nominal 29,000, though some of the lower stands have been closed off against better days ahead.

Birmingham City's most famous player is probably Trevor Francis, who was sadly to die young a few months later, though my friend John who is steeped in 1950s football might vote for Gil Merrick. But Jude Bellingham has the promise to surpass the achievements of those two, and he was introduced to the crowd, having just starred in the recently finished World Cup. He was making his first visit to the ground since leaving for Borussia Dortmund.

It was a bumper year for minutes of silence, with the death of the Queen added to the usual Remembrance Day tributes, and commemorations of local worthies who had passed on. This evening's tribute was particularly moving, as it was in memory of four small boys who had tragically died after falling through ice into a freezing pond.

Troy Deeney is one football's good guys and was playing his 600th game. Peter Crouch is famous for his answer to the standard question 'What would you have been if you weren't a footballer?' 'A virgin.' Troy's answer to the same question is more socially relevant – 'Probably a drug dealer'.

Anyway his milestone match got off to the best possible start, as he smartly put away a through pass in the second minute. He followed this up by winning a penalty and converting it emphatically. Matters got worse for Reading when a defensive error let in Curacao born Tahith Chong to round the goalkeeper and add a third.

Reading's Paul Ince responded with several substitutions, including Andy Carroll, Junior Hoilett, and Angola international Lucas Joao. They made a brief rally at the end, finally beating John Ruddy twice, but the goals were too late to affect the result. Bellingham's talented 17 year old brother Jobe came on for Birmingham for the last 15 minutes.

The win lifted Birmingham above Reading, into 7th place, just below the play-off positions.

Birmingham City 3 (Deeney 1, 23p, Chong 36) Reading 2 (Lucas Joao 83, Ince 90+4) Attendance 14,627

45. Coventry City v Swansea City

17 December 2022 – Coventry Building Society Arena – EFL Championship

I drove to Coventry the next morning, and had time to visit the iconic Cathedral. I followed this with a humungus fry-up, consuming a month's ration of cholesterol.

I'd been to Coventry's old ground at Highfield Road during Manchester City's abortive title challenge in 1974, when the team was destabilised by the signing of Rodney Marsh. In 2005 Coventry moved to the Coventry Building Society Arena, then known as the Ricoh stadium, but fell into financial difficulties and, at times, had to ground share and play at Northampton Town's Sixfields or Birmingham's St Andrews. Earlier that week Coventry had secured a rental agreement with the new owners of the CBS Arena and could now finally call it home. It's a fairly nondescript out of town stadium, on the A464 and just off the M6.

This match featured two fairly mid table teams. Coventry's manager was Mark Robbins, whose 1990 FA Cup goal against Nottingham Forest allegedly saved Alex Ferguson's career at Manchester United.

Jonathan Panzo, on loan from Nottingham Forest, headed in a first senior goal before second-half goals from Jamie Allen and Swedish international Viktor Gyokeres put Coventry 3-0 ahead after 54 minutes. Joel Piroe got one back for Swansea 14 minutes later from close range and then, shortly after, Jay Fulton made it 3-2. Coventry were suddenly hanging on and, amid growing excitement, Liam Cullen scored a tap in six minutes from time to complete a most improbable comeback.

'20 minutes ago we were 8th, now we're now 14th' lamented a Coventry supporter on the way out.

Coventry City 3 (Panzo 29, Allen 47, Gyokeres 54)
Swansea City 3 (Piroe 68, Fulton 76, Cullen 84)
Attendance 17,905

46. MK Dons v Leicester City

20 December 2022 – MK Stadium – Carabao
Cup Round 3

The World Cup had just finished, and the League managed to squeeze in the third round of the Carabao Cup into the few days before Christmas. En route to MK Dons I spent an afternoon at nearby Bletchley Park, where I enjoyed the exhibits describing the wartime exploits of the World War 2 code breakers. There was one display showing the names of those from Oxford and Cambridge who had worked there. Alan Turing, who went to my old college, was the most famous, but there were also several other names who I remember from my time there in the 1960s.

The MK Stadium, built in 2007 next to a big shopping and restaurant complex, holds an ambitious 30,000, but it was half empty that night. MK Dons were thoroughly outgunned by their Premier League opponents. Leicester played Tielemans, who had played for Belgium in the World Cup, but curiously rested Maddison, who hadn't kicked a ball for England. Tielemans opened the scoring after the Dons keeper had saved an audacious flick from Vardy. Their second came after Ayoza Perez showed great skill to bring down a high ball, and Vardy sealed the match, nodding home a cross just after half time.

Jamie will have been glad to be on the pitch, to escape his family courtroom drama 'Rooney v Vardy' which was being aired on Channel Four.

MK Dons 0 Leicester City 3 (Tielemans 18, Perez 29 Vardy 50)
Attendance 15,495

47. Charlton Athletic v Brighton & HA

21 December 2022 – Valley Stadium – Carabao Cup Round 3

The start of the second half of my 92 grounds was another Carabao Cup match. What should have been a straightforward train journey to Charlton was stymied by yet another rail strike and I endured a grim car journey of almost two hours round the M25. The ground at The Valley has had a chequered history, having fallen into disrepair in the late 1980s, causing Charlton to have to ground share first at Crystal Palace then at West Ham. It was rebuilt and reopened in 1992, since which many improvements have been made.

Since their FA Cup loss at Stockport Charlton were languishing 18th in League One, and had appointed Dean Holden as their manager the day before, their fifth manager in two years. This should have been a walk for Brighton, but of course with the World Cup they hadn't played for seven weeks. Lallana skimmed the bar early on, but no goals came. De Zerbi sent on the cavalry in the second half in the shape of Mitoma, Trossard, and Estupian. There was mild amusement as one of the Charlton subs got injured after only 5 minutes on the pitch, but still no goals, though March dribbled through and shot wide.

The penalty shootout had a farcical start. Gross hit the left hand post with the first, then Charlton's Stockley hit the other post, before Trossard completed the full set by hitting the crossbar. Charlton missed two more, so Solly March had the fifth penalty to win for Brighton. He shot high into the stand, so it went to sudden death. Both teams scored their sixth, then Caicedo missed for Brighton and Sam Lavelle scored to put Charlton into the quarter finals.

'We hope the M23 is closed' chortled the Charlton fans unsympathetically as we left the ground. Luckily at the late hour I had a shorter drive home through central London. Charlton's reward was a quarter final at Old Trafford, where they were knocked out by a goal from Antony and two from Rashford. A few months later Solly March was to repeat his skied penalty against Manchester United, a miss which cost his team an FA Cup final appearance.

Charlton Athletic 0 Brighton & HA 0
(Charlton won 4-3 on penalties)
Attendance 17,464

48. Barnsley v Fleetwood Town

29 December 2022 – Oakwell Stadium – League
One

I took a short break to spend Christmas Day and Boxing Day with my son Tim in Barcelona, where it was mild enough to swim (briefly!) in the Mediterranean on Christmas Day. So there was quite a temperature contrast when I headed north for a couple of League One matches.

The first was at Barnsley, one of those towns you wouldn't visit without a good reason. Even the local museum was closed for the Christmas break. Furthermore, it is an Uber free town, and I was staying far enough from the ground to need taxis. Fortunately a local firm, Blue Line Taxis, was excellent.

Oakwell is an ancient ground which Barnsley had to sell to the council in 2003 when it went into administration. The club owned a lot of land around it which has now been redeveloped to include facilities for the academy and some training pitches.

Barnsley bossed the first half without scoring. They took the lead after 64 minutes with a fierce shot into the roof of the net from a narrow angle on the left, but then conceded a penalty, awarded for a clumsy challenge on the splendidly named Admiral Muskwe, a Zimbabwean international on loan from Luton. Muskwe himself converted for Fleetwood. A few minutes from time Barnsley were denied a strong appeal for a penalty themselves. This lead to a chaotic melee, and manager Michael Duff was sent to the stands. The incident had a happy ending for Barnsley though, as from the resulting corner defender Robbie

Cundy scored with an unstoppable header. Barnsley saw out a tense six minutes of stoppage time to seal a win which kept them in the playoff places.

**Barnsley 2 (Norwood 64, Cundy 86) Fleetwood Town 1
(Muskwe 77p)
Attendance 10,219**

49. Lincoln City v Bolton Wanderers

30 December 2022 – LNER Stadium (Sincil Bank) – League One

By train from Barnsley via Sheffield to the pretty city of Lincoln. Although it is inland, the centre of the city is made more attractive by having several developments on the waterways created by the River Witham. By reason of its geography Lincolnshire played a major part in the World War 2 air war, including the legendary Dambusters raid. There is a Bomber Command Visitors Centre just outside Lincoln covering this which I wanted to see. Unfortunately, after a stiff uphill walk of over a mile, I discovered that it was closed for a private function. So I went back into town and looked round Lincoln Cathedral which, as anyone who does pub quizzes will know, overtook the Great Pyramid of Giza to become the tallest building in the world when its central spire was completed in 1311.

The attractively named Sincil Bank, 'Sinny Bank' to the locals, has been Lincoln's home since 1895, though they have had to sell it and lease it back. Sponsorship necessity means that it is now officially and prosaically called the LNER Stadium. I was in the short queue to enter when my phone beeped with a news flash. Pele had died. I was lucky enough to see him once, playing in a friendly for Santos at Fulham, and was proud to join the minute's applause which was held.

The visitors Bolton were in the play-off spots, and had caused a heavy police presence by bringing 1200 spectators. They fell behind when they were caught napping by a quickly taken free kick giving Lincoln's striker Ben House a simple chance. Bolton missed a couple of good chances before equalising early in the second half when former Derry City defender Eoin Toal headed in from a corner – his first goal for the club, and Bolton's only shot on target. Bolton will have fancied their chances of winning when Lincoln's Joe Walsh collected two yellow cards within four minutes, but the ten men held on for a draw.

Back on the train the next morning in time for New Year's Eve festivities.

Lincoln City 1 (House 10) Bolton Wanderers 1 (Toal 58)
Attendance 9,047

50. Millwall v Rotherham United

1 January 2023 – The New Den – EFL Championship

It was a bit of a struggle to get out of bed after celebrating New Year's Eve, but at least the drive through London to Millwall was quiet.

I'd been to the New Den in the 1990s when Manchester City were languishing in the lower leagues. The away fans were kept in for an hour after the final whistle, a serious inconvenience for a midweek evening fixture. Built in 1993, it is Millwall's sixth ground. It has a charming memorial area where supporters have put up plaques to commemorate fans who have died – 'In loving memory of Denis, lifelong Lions fans, loving granddad and dad'. There was an exception to the stereotype of the Millwall fan –'nobody loves us, and we don't care'. As I took my seat the chap seated behind me solemnly stood up, shook my hand, and wished me a happy new year.

Millwall, managed by Gary Rowett, were in contention for the Championship play-offs, and scored first when their Welsh striker Tom Bradshaw jumped highest to head in a free kick. They missed a couple of chances to increase their lead but, before the break, Rotherham missed the best chance of the match. Their Northern Ireland international striker Conor Washington was put clean through on goal, rounded the goalkeeper and then managed to shoot over the bar. This was the closest Rotherham came to scoring. Bradshaw created the second goal with a shot which went in off a defender, and added a third ten minutes from time.

The win put Millwall above Luton on goal difference, and left Rotherham one point above the relegation

Millwall 3 (Bradshaw 4, 81 Humphreys og 66)
Rotherham United 0
Attendance 12,899

51. Northampton Town v Leyton Orient

2 January 2023 – Sixfields Stadium – League Two

Northampton Town used to share their ground with the county cricket club, but moved in 1994 to Sixfields – a pleasant stadium whose main stand looks as if built with Meccano.

It was a nice afternoon for a top of the table clash – the teams being third and first in League Two. The first half was mostly notable for the number of stoppages. There were three injury substitutions and players have learnt that they can cause an instant stoppage by going down holding their head.

The deadlock was broken early in the second half when Northampton's Ben Fox scored after a brilliant save by the Orient keeper. A few minutes later Orient looked to have equalised when Grenada international Omar Beckles had the ball in the net. It looked offside from where I sat but the linesman kept his flag down. The crowd erupted in protest and the referee had a long consultation with him, before he appeared to overrule him and disallow the goal.

With 7 minutes stoppage time added, Orient had a free kick from which a Northampton player went down clutching his face. 'Elbow' screamed the fans. Everyone on the field was putting his oar in but to great booing, then ref only gave a yellow card to Beckles. Both linesmen intervened and after further interminable discussion, the card was upgraded to red.

Northampton hung on for their win and the game finally ended at ten past five. Much of the stoppage time was due to indecisive officiating, and allowing an unseemly level of protest. Orient stayed on top of the table, despite receiving only their third defeat of the season.

I'd parked in a nearby muddy field (Seventh Field?) which the attendant who took my £3 said closed at 5.30. Cars were still making their way out at 6pm.

Northampton Town 1 (Fox 51) Leyton Orient 0
Attendance 7,475

52. Southampton v Nottingham Forest

4 January 2023 – St Mary's Stadium – Premier League

I've been a frequent visitor to St Mary's, and its predecessor The Dell. My friend Dave has been a Saints supporter since childhood and kindly let me use a spare family season ticket, so I travelled down with him and his wife Liz, an equally keen supporter. Southampton had had a bad run and sacked manager Ralf Hasenhuttl a month earlier. His replacement Nathan Jones, who had come from Luton, had lost his first four matches, so that Saints were propping up the table. Forest were one place above them and had gained only two points away from home, scoring only one away goal, yes only one! So the contest was a real 'six-pointer'.

Southampton's real problem lack of a striker was amply illustrated early on when Che Adams shot wide when clean through. At the other end Brennan Johnson hit the bar with a similar chance. Then Forest took the lead, doubling their away goal total in the process. It was a dreadfully soft goal, given away by a sloppy pass which allowed Johnson to run through and set up the Nigerian international Awoniyi with a tap in. 'How shit must you be, we're winning away' chortled the large Forest following.

Southampton were predictably booed off at half time. They played more positively in the second half but Ward-Prowse couldn't make any impression and Southampton didn't even manage a shot on target. Forest climbed from 19th to 15th and I wondered if I hadn't seen two teams both heading for relegation. The drive back up the M3 was very quiet.

Southampton 0 Nottingham Forest 1 (Awoniyi 27)
Attendance 30,150

53. Crystal Palace v Southampton

7 January 2023 – Selhurst Park – FA Cup Round 3

Barely 48 hours after watching their defeat to Nottingham Forest, I was watching them again at Crystal Palace in the FA Cup third round, the ticket again kindly procured by Dave. With my son Tim being a Palace supporter, I've always enjoyed going to Selhurst Park, a cosy ground with lots of atmosphere.

Crystal Palace have recently depended a lot on the skills of Wilfrid Zaha, and he was instrumental in setting up their opener. His through pass found Odsonne Edouard, whose fierce shot went in despite Saints keeper Bazunu getting a hand to it. It could easily have been 2-0 when Jordan Ayew rattled the crossbar. Southampton's go-to player for many seasons has been James Ward-Prowse, whose direct free kicks have been a lucrative source of goals. This one was from far out on the left, and intended as a cross. But nobody connected, and Palace's Guaita reacted too late to prevent the ball sneaking in. Guiata was even more at fault for the decisive goal. He dawdled on the ball just outside his area, and Adam Armstrong charged down his clearance and was left with an open goal.

The match ended with predictable booing, and I couldn't help thinking that Southampton would have preferred their last two results to be reversed. Their cup run was brought to an embarrassing end in the fifth round by a home defeat to Grimsby. For some reason the attendance was never published.

**Crystal Palace 1 (Edouard 14) Southampton 2
(Ward-Prowse 37, Armstrong 68)**

54. Bristol City v Swansea City

8 January 2023 – Ashton Gate – FA Cup Round 3

Bristol City share their Ashton Gate ground with Bristol Bears Rugby Club, and it is one of the nicest grounds I visited, set near a shopping centre. There is a statue to the club's most famous son, John Atyeo, and easy access to a spacious food/drink area, with an excellent selection. Swansea brought over 2000 supporters to add some Welsh fervour to this cup-tie.

Less than 24 hours after Crystal Palace gave away a soft goal to lose to Southampton, Bristol exhibited the same death wish. After 20 minutes, a loose pass was pounced on and squared for Dutch striker Carl Piroe to give Swansea an early lead. They were playing the better football, with Joe Allen pulling the strings after his spell with Wales at the World Cup. Bristol tried to up the tempo, and had a couple of what seemed reasonable shouts for a penalty turned down by Craig Pawson – an excellent referee whose calm demeanour seems to discourage excessive protests.

Bristol are captained by Austrian international Andreas Weimann, who has anglicised his handle to 'Andi'. I didn't notice him till early in the second half, when he sent a wayward shot into row Z. But 15 minutes from time, he hit a long cross into the Swansea area and Semenyo, who had been in the Ghana World Cup squad, headed the equaliser and sent the tie to a replay, which Bristol City won 2-1 after extra time.

Bristol City 1 (Semenyo 75) Swansea City 1 (Piroe 15)
Attendance 21,007

55. Bradford City v Rochdale

10 January 2023 – Bradford University Stadium
(Valley Parade) – League Two

Apart from its football team and legacy of closed woollen mills, Bradford is home to the National Science and Media museum. Overlooked by a huge statue to Bradford's famous son J B Priestley, this contains, among other artefacts, the world's oldest negative, dating from 1835.

It was a filthy day and I made the half hour walk to Valley Parade in pouring rain. The old stadium achieved notoriety in 1985 for the dreadful fire which killed 56 people. I was working in Kuwait at the time, and for weeks the national TV station played as a backdrop to the closing news headlines footage of the fire which was far too graphic to be shown in the UK. The rain made the pitch a bit unpredictable – 'like an Indian test wicket' said the bloke behind me. Trust a Yorkshireman to express it in cricketing terms.

Bradford City were lying in a playoff spot, faced Rochdale who had climbed one place from the bottom since I saw them four months earlier. Bradford had an old favourite in the dugout – Mark Hughes (whose first name is actually Leslie)

Playing in their distinctive brown and yellow stripes, Bradford took the lead on the half hour, when the Sudanese Abo Soisa cleverly slipped his marker and shot home. Rochdale hit the post with a free kick but Bradford remained in control until well into the second half, when in a rare attack, Rochdale were awarded a penalty. I didn't get a good look, but the fans around me were incensed. The kick was saved but Rochdale's Ian Henderson followed up and scored from the rebound. The whole tone of the match changed and a few minutes later Henderson, who was a few weeks short of his 38th birthday, scored what proved to be the winner when he turned in a cross from close range. Despite the entreaties of the crowd, Sparky seemed reluctant to use his substitutes until almost the end.

This was Rochdale's second win of the season and I hoped it would be the launch pad for them to avoid playing Altrincham in the National League next year. But it wasn't to be.

Bradford City 1 (Eisa 29) Rochdale 2 (Henderson 63, 70)
Attendance 17,061

56. Mansfield Town v Crewe Alexandra

14 January 2023 – One Call Stadium (Field Mill) – League Two

Next I embarked on a long driving trip up north taking in four matches in four days. First came a schlep up the M1 to Mansfield. I set off early as I wanted to watch the Manchester derby which kicked off at 12.30. This was a big match for City as, against most expectations, Arsenal still held the lead in the Premier League they had taken at the end of August. City were leading 1-0 when, 12 minutes from time, Casemiro played a through ball to Marcus Rashford, who was in an offside position. Realising this, Rashford didn't play the ball, but ran alongside it until Fernandes arrived and shot past the understandably distracted Ederson. A lengthy VAR review allowed the goal to stand, as Rashford hadn't touched the ball. A clear illustration of the letter of the law taking priority over common sense. And of course United went on to score a second a few minutes later.

So I was in a bad mood as I walked to Field Mill (aka the One Call Stadium), another ground with only three sides. Mansfield, who play in a natty yellow and amber, are known as the Stags because of the proximity of Sherwood forest. They were managed by another golden oldie, Nigel Clough. They scored first when midfielder George Maris poked home a cross from close range, but gave up their lead just after half time when a loose pass was seized upon by Crewe defender Kelvin Mellor, who scored with a thumping 30 yard shot. Mansfield had the better of the play after that until Mellor was sent off late on. The foul was committed quite far out but the referee, to my surprise, judged it a denial of a goal scoring opportunity – a 'Dogso' in refereeing jargon. 'Get up you jelly-legged twat' yelled the bloke next to me. Thereafter Mansfield's ten men held on for the draw which left them in 7th place.

Mansfield Town 1 (Maris 42) Crewe Alexandra 1 (Mellor 50)
Attendance 6,142

57. Newcastle United v Fulham

15 January 2023 – St James Park – Premier
League

This was a Sunday lunchtime kick-off. I met up for a drink with
my friend Andrew, a Newcastle season ticket holder, who had
kindly procured me a ticket in the away end from a Fulham
supporter. Another Fulham faithful Harry, a school friend
of Adam, turned up with a couple of spare tickets as a couple
of his mates had got into a scrap while sampling Newcastle's
famous night life, and had spent the night as a guest of the local
constabulary.

The atmosphere at St James Park has always been legendary,
and the excitement had gone up a notch since the Saudi takeover
and their improved results. The away supporters' area is at the
far end, very high up, with a fabulous view over the city. Eddie
Howe played Joelinton despite the player having been stopped
for drink driving on the previous Thursday. The first half was
relatively quiet with Callum Wilson having the best chances.
The game came to life in the 67th minute, when a VAR review
determined that a foul by Trippier had been just inside the area.
There were then usual silly shenanigans in the penalty area
which resulted in Pope being booked before Mitrovic stepped
up and scored. Except he hadn't. He'd slipped and the ball had
deflected off his standing foot. No goal, free kick to Newcastle.
The final quarter was frantic, with both teams attacking.

The deciding goal came at the death. Longstaff's cross
was stood up at the back post by Wilson and Alexander Isak,

Newcastle's most expensive signing, playing his first game for four months, headed in from a yard. Cue absolute bedlam and Newcastle were third in the table.

A couple of hours later I watched on TV as Arsenal beat Tottenham 2-0 to increase their lead over Manchester City.

Newcastle United 1 (Isak 89) Fulham 0
Attendance 52,247

58. Port Vale v Peterborough United

16 January 2023 – Vale Park – League One

I had a very scenic drive south to the Potteries, especially on the M62 over the snow-capped Pennines. The ending was less scenic – Burslem, which would be a candidate for the hose if England needed an enema. To add to my impression of the place, Booking.com had booked me into a hotel which had clearly closed for business ages ago, forcing me to get a room next to the Stoke City ground.

Port Vale play at Vale Park, which was built in 1950. Remarkably, it once held just under 50,000 for an FA Cup tie against Aston Villa, but it is now a tired ground, which holds about 15,000.

On this freezing night, it was only about one third full. After a dull first half in front of the Sky cameras, I spent the whole break walking up and down to thaw out my feet. Ephron Mason-Clark put Darren Ferguson's side ahead after 56 minutes with a close range back post header and made the game safe when he added a second 8 minutes later, also from short range, a result which left Peterborough in 7th place.

I have used Booking.com extensively in my travels, but on this occasion the company didn't cover itself in glory. Months later, I lost the will to live trying to get a refund for the non-existent room they had charged me for, as they simply kept referring me back to the non-existent hotel.

Port Vale 0 Peterborough United 2 (Mason-Clark 56, 64)
Attendance 5,109

59. Wigan Athletic v Luton Town

20 January 2023 – DW Stadium – FA Cup Round 3 Replay

From the Potteries I drove north for lunch with some cousins at Ainsdale, on the golf course coast north of Liverpool, before heading to Wigan for an FA Cup replay.

The DW Stadium, named after Dave Whelan who owned Wigan at the time, was built in 1999 and is a multi-purpose facility. Wigan Athletic shares the ground with Wigan Warriors Rugby League club, and one of the stands is named after the legendary Billy Boston.

The third round replay took place on another freezing night, after the match at Luton had ended 1-1. Since I had last watched Luton, manager Nathan Jones had left for Southampton, and they had benefitted from the Watford merry-go-round by recruiting Rob Edwards. They came into the game off the back of a defeat by West Brom in the Championship where they squandered a two goal lead to lose 3-2. Wigan had another old favourite in the dugout – Kolo Toure, formerly of Arsenal, Manchester City and Liverpool.

The only incident of note in the first half was that it snowed. Immediately after half time Wigan broke the deadlock with a fine 20 yard volley, but Luton hit back within five minutes with a scrappy scrambled goal. They did more pressing after that, and I confess to some relief at being spared a cold extra time when, 8 minutes into stoppage time, Luton's Adebayo took the ball with his back to goal and performed a smart turn to score the winner to leave the home crowd deflated.

Wigan Athletic 1 (Aasgard 46) Luton Town 2 (Woodrow 51, Adebayo 90+8)
Attendance 5,668

60. Sheffield United v Hull City

20 January 2023 – Bramall Lane – EFL
Championship

My second visit to Sheffield was for a Friday evening match, and gave me a chance to visit the city's Millennium Gallery in the afternoon. Situated in a shopping mall, this has some fine seascapes, an exhibition of the work of John Ruskin, and some fascinating metalwork illustrating the city's history of steelmaking.

Sheffield United has played at Bramall Lane since 1889. It is a venerable stadium, originally a cricket ground at which Yorkshire played till 1973, and which hosted an Ashes test in 1902.

Burnley and Sheffield United had opened up a significant gap at the top of the Championship, and the opposition being Hull ensured a big ground and a heavy police presence. The crowd gave a brief rendition of their famous Chip Butty song before kick-off, and they soon had something to cheer about when Canadian born Daniel Jebbison latched onto a through pass and scored for the Blades. There were chances at both ends, with Hull's Oscar Estupinan going closest. My seat was in the front row and I had a good view of Hull coach Liam Rosenior responding to some gentle abuse by blowing the spectators a kiss. Manchester City loanee Tommy Doyle made a good impression before he was substituted after 70 minutes. Shortly before the end there was a melee at a corner which resulted in Hull's substitute Tetteh getting a straight red card. I didn't get a good view but apparently it was for a head butt. The 1-0 win meant that Sheffield had opened up a 14 point lead over the third place club, and looked odds on for promotion.

I'd planned to go to nearby Doncaster the following day but it was announced that their match was postponed due to a frozen pitch. So with some rapid re-planning, I booked to go and watch Grimsby v Harrogate. I was sitting on the train meandering through the Lincolnshire countryside at about midday when I detected some chatter among the handful of Harrogate supporters. They had heard that this match too was off, news which the Harrogate fans took remarkably calmly. It was too late to rebook my train home, so I spent a couple of hours at the Fisheries Heritage Museum. Incidentally, and counter intuitively, Grimsby is north of Sheffield.

Sheffield United 1 (Jeppison 4) Hull City 0
Attendance 29,271

61. Ipswich Town v Morecambe

24 January 2023 – Portman Road – League One

Strangely I'd never been to Ipswich before, and a Tuesday evening match gave me the chance to look around. I spent the afternoon visiting Christchurch Manor – a fine Tudor mansion with an excellent collection of paintings, lots of Constable of course and several Manets and Pissarros. I then walked down to the elegant waterfront redevelopment on the banks of the River Orwell.

The short walk from my hotel took me over the Sir Bobby Robson footbridge to Portman Road, where a healthy crowd came to support Ipswich's bid for promotion to the Championship. They couldn't have had a better start. An attack forcing a corner, and a goal from striker Freddie Ladapo. 1-0 after 52 seconds. Five minutes later a powerful 20 yard shot whacked against the post, and ten minutes after that, Ladapo doubled his tally and Ipswich's lead. Ipswich continued to dominate and at the end of the half added two more through Conor Chaplin.

The second half was just as one sided as Morecambe, who didn't muster a shot on target, largely conceded the mid field to Ipswich. But despite several good chances, there were no more goals. The result put Ipswich into third place, and left Morecambe precariously placed in the drop zone.

A particular shout out to their 102 fans who braved the cold night and will have faced a fairly miserable 280 mile journey back to Morecambe.

Ipswich Town 4 (Ladapo 1, 16, Chaplin 36, 45+6)
Morecambe 0
Attendance 21,948

62. Shrewsbury Town v Forest Green Rovers

28 January 2023 – Montgomery Waters Meadow – League One

As everybody over a certain age knows, Shrewsbury used to play at the splendidly named Gay Meadow, but about 15 years ago the new Montgomery Waters Meadow stadium was opened. This is a pleasant ground, but a couple of miles out of town.

Forest Green Rovers were firmly anchored at the bottom of League One, and had just changed their manager, so that the unmistakeable shirt sleeved figure of Duncan Ferguson was prowling in the dugout – his first full time managerial appointment. His reign got off to a great start when a stunning strike from outside the area by Jordon Garrick, on loan from Swansea, gave them the lead.

After that the match was fairly even and after the 90 minutes the fourth official advised there would be six minutes added time, continuing the trend started at the World Cup for longer stoppage time. At this point a player went down with a head injury. These things can take a while, so I decided to leave then as I had a long walk back to the station. But before I left the stadium, there was a roar. Shrewsbury had equalised. And shortly afterwards another roar indicated a late winner. Bad timing!

This unfortunate start to Big Dunc's managerial appointment was as close as he got to a win for several months. FGR won only one of their remaining 14 matches, and were duly relegated back to League Two after only one season. And inevitably, they parted company with Ferguson.

Shrewsbury Town 2 (Pyke 90+4, Bowman 90+8)
Forest Green Rovers 1 (Garrick 18)
Attendance 6,310

63. Derby County v West Ham United

20 January 2023 – Pride Park Stadium – FA Cup Round 4

My next trip took me to Derby and Carlisle, a journey I had to drive because of yet another day of industrial disruption on the railways. My hotel in Derby had a nice view of the River Derwent, alongside which I walked to Pride Park, which had replaced the Baseball ground in 1997.

This was a Monday evening 4th round FA Cup match on BBC. There were several thousand away fans who added to the atmosphere, and West Ham fielded a pretty strong team, although with Declan Rice on the bench. The only Derby players I had heard of were the veteran Curtis Davies and Irish internationals James Collins and Conor Hourihane.

West Ham were too close to relegation for comfort and manager David Moyes was considered under pressure, so it was a relief for him when they took the lead after ten minutes. A neat move, Soucek to Antonio, back to Soucek, who headed across goal for Bowen to finish. 'Your ground's too big for you', sang the West Ham fans. 'Your ground's a running track' retorted the home supporters. West Ham doubled their lead early in the second half when Bowen's cross deflected off a defender straight into the path of Antonio, who couldn't miss. 'We'll never play you again' sang the away fans, as Derby brought on Jake Rooney, Wayne's cousin. West Ham earned a fifth round trip to Old Trafford, where they lead until the 77th minute before losing 3-1.

Back at my hotel the bar was full of West Ham fans. The main topic of conversation was where Declan Rice would go in the summer. The consensus, correctly as it turned out, was Arsenal.

Derby County 0 West Ham United 2 (Bowen 10, Antonio 50)
Attendance 25,308

64. Carlisle United v Barrow

31 January 2023 – Brunton Road – League Two

En route to Carlisle I spent some time in the quaint market town of Penrith. My father was born in Carlisle in 1917, and I looked up his birthplace. The address was in Warwick Road, which is now better described as the A69 Carlisle to Newcastle road. I rang the bell and the owner kindly invited me into his splendid Victorian house, which is a few hundred yards from Carlisle United's Brunton Park. The whole area has had two catastrophic floods in the last decade, and the water had filled the ground floor to a depth of 3 or 4 feet. The owner had taken advantage of his insurance pay out to make some lovely improvements, and he showed me the amazing precautions he had now taken against a recurrence. He reckoned that the minimum claim in his street had been £100,000.

Brunton Park has a bar named after Chris Balderstone, who made history by being the last person to play professional cricket and football on the same day. In September 1975, he was 51 not out for Leicestershire against Derbyshire at Chesterfield at close of play, changed into football kit, played at Doncaster in a 1-1 draw against Brentford, and returned to Chesterfield next morning to complete his century!

Barrow is 50 miles away from Carlisle, but this fixture is called 'The Cumbria Derby'. Last year's fixture was almost abandoned after a firework was thrown at the goalkeeper, and there was a big crowd and plenty of police. Carlisle, challenging for promotion, were managed by Paul Simpson who played for Manchester City in the 1980s. They didn't score until just before half time, but added four more in the second half, one from 34 year-old midfielder Joe Garner who was in his fourth spell at the club. Barrow got a slightly comical own goal as a late consolation, but Carlisle added a fifth in stoppage from the penalty spot after their striker rounded the Barrow goalkeeper and was tripped when about to score.

The following morning I had time to look round Carlisle Castle and Cathedral before the long drive south.

Carlisle United 5 (Mellish 44, 67, Garner 50, Patrick 72, Dennis 89p) Barrow 1 (Barclay 84og)
Attendance 9,351

65. Swansea City v Birmingham City

4 February 2023 – Swansea.com (Liberty) Stadium – EFL Championship

The rail journey from Reading to Swansea would have been more comfortable had it not clashed with the opening Six Nations rugby match in Cardiff, though luckily I did get a seat in both directions. The department of silly names had chosen the Swansea.com Stadium for the ground that had opened in 2005 as the Liberty Stadium. Or perhaps more politically correctly the Stadiwm Swansea.com

My friend and ex work colleague Neil had kindly procured me a seat in the away end, and I was rewarded with my most exciting match to date. After they had brought a couple of saves from John Ruddy, Swansea gifted the first goal by failing to deal with a bouncing ball and conceding a penalty which their keeper nearly saved. They then recovered well to lead 2-1 at half time. After Birmingham brought it back to 2-2, Swansea went ahead 3-2 when Ruddy made a horrible mess of a clearance and presented Dutch striker Joel Piroe with his second goal. Swansea then had the misfortune to lose a player to injury when they had used all their substitutes, so had to finish with 10 men. Birmingham took advantage of the extra man and scrambled an equaliser from a deflected header. There were 7 minutes of added time. Birmingham forced a corner right at the death, and the American Auston Trusty lived up to his name by heading the winner. Cue noisy scenes in the away end, though I felt Swansea were a little unlucky.

There was time before my train back to watch some of the England v Scotland rugby international from Twickenham, before a journey home accompanied by many boisterous Irishmen who had seen their team beat Wales at the Millennium Stadium.

Swansea City 3 (Piroe 23, 58 Cullen 29) Birmingham City 4 (Hogan 14p, Chong 55, Jutkiewicz 90, Trusty 90+7) Attendance 17,247

66. Blackburn Rovers v Wigan Athletic

6 February 2023 – Ewood Park – EFL Championship

I now had three matches in the north, beginning at Blackburn. My maternal grandfather was born there in 1885 and, after passing a fine statue of Gladstone, I sought out the house in Wellington Road where he lived his early life. The demographics of Blackburn have changed a little since then, and situated opposite now is the Mohaddis-e-Azam Education Centre.

Ewood Park is reached from town by walking along the Leeds to Liverpool canal. It originally opened in 1882, and I had been there once when I was young. It has since been completely transformed by the money injected into the club in the 1990s by Jack Walker, after whom a stand is named. Aficionados of the 1960s will approve of the fact that other stands are named after Ronnie Clayton and Bryan Douglas, but I was not reassured by a sign which said 'Danger Fragile Roof'.

My first reaction when the teams came out was to look for Kolo Toure in the Wigan dugout, but he had been fired after only nine games in charge and replaced a few days earlier by Scottish international Shaun Maloney, who had played for Wigan in their historic 2013 FA Cup Final victory over Manchester City.

The match was a fairly unremarkable 0-0 draw, though Wigan did come close when Omar Rekik, on loan from Arsenal, shot narrowly wide, and they bundled home a corner only to be penalised for a foul on the goalkeeper. Blackburn had missed out on a couple of signings on deadline day due to incorrect documentation, and will have regarded this as a missed opportunity, while Wigan's point wasn't enough to lift them off the bottom.

I had a narrow escape when I contrived to let my phone fall from my pocket but luckily someone handed it to a helpful steward. Life would have been interesting without it, as I was staying in an unmanned hotel which could only be accessed by app! And as a secondary escape, I only missed by a day Tony Blackburn hosting a 1950s music evening.

Blackburn Rovers 0   Wigan Athletic 0
Attendance 14,540

67. Doncaster Rovers v Tranmere Rovers

7 February 2023 – Ecopower Stadium
(Keepmoat) – League Two

The train journey from Blackburn to Doncaster involved a change at Leeds and the first leg went through Hebden Bridge, which was featuring on many TV screens at the time as the location for the drama Happy Valley. My preconception of Doncaster related to steel, coal mining and the St Leger, but a couple of miles out of town is a very pleasant lake near which the ground is situated. Near this lake is also the South Yorkshire Aircraft Museum, a haven for aircraft aficionados, containing a random collection of old aircraft and helicopters, engines, and other parts such as cockpits, instruments and seats, including a some planes which had seen service in the Falklands war.

The Keepmoat Stadium, built in 2006, is part of a larger sports complex, and now sponsored as the Eco-Power Stadium. It is an excellent facility which is also used by Doncaster Rugby League Club, and the Doncaster Belles ladies team. It has a splendid feature – an indoor bar under the stand with plenty of seating where spectators can enjoy a drink until about two minutes before kick-off. A most welcome facility on a cold February evening.

This was a match between two mid table teams. Someone in Tranmere's marketing department had decided that their away kit should be a fetching peppermint green. Tranmere had the better of the first hour, forcing a couple of smart saves from the Doncaster goalkeeper, but fell behind after 62 minutes when a speculative shot took a wicked deflection. A couple of minutes later a defender dawdled on the ball and Doncaster added a second. Tranmere hit the bar towards the end, but the game finished 2-0, and I took the chance to return to the Belle Vue bar to thaw out.

Doncaster Rovers 2 (Close 62, Hurst 65) Tranmere Rovers 0
Attendance 5,775

68. Sunderland v Fulham

8 February 2023 – Stadium of Light – FA Cup Round 4 Replay

A lunchtime arrival from Doncaster gave me a free afternoon in Sunderland which I spent visiting the National Glass Centre, which is reached by a pleasant walk along the River Wear. This contains some beautiful pieces of glass artwork, and there was the obligatory demonstration of glass blowing – a skill which never ceases to fascinate me. Sunderland's industrial heritage is mainly associated with ship building, but in the 1870s the city also produced one third of England's sheet glass.

I had been to the Stadium of Light once before. My family history research revealed that a great uncle, Alex Barrie, had been a professional footballer for Kilmarnock, Rangers and Sunderland before the Great War, and that he apparently had the distinction of being the second player ever to be sent off for Sunderland. Sadly he was killed in France only a month before the armistice. I contacted the club about this connection in 2019 and they kindly invited me to lay a wreath and watch a match. I had a memorable evening, hosted by their legendary goalkeeper Jim Montgomery, whose moment of fame was a spectacular double save in one of the greatest cup upsets of all time – Sunderland's 1-0 win over Leeds in the 1973 cup final. Outside the Stadium of Light there is a statue depicting Bob Stokoe, their manager that day, as he ran onto the pitch at the final whistle.

This evening's match promised to be a cracker after the teams had drawn 1-1 at Craven Cottage. With Fulham making nine changes the home supporters had good reason to feel optimistic. But Harry Wilson gave Fulham an early lead with a clever finish using the outside of his left foot. He might well have had two more before half-time but the score remained 1-0. Then Marco Silva, who was watching from a TV gantry having picked up four yellow cards, decided to strengthen Fulham by bringing on Mitrovic and Pereira. The change soon paid dividends when Mitrovic set up a second for Pereira. Sunderland's Clarke then hit back with an excellent angled shot. This had the large crowd bouncing but Fulham soon silenced them by restoring their two goal advantage through left back Kurzawa. There was time for one last flourish from Sunderland when Costa Rican substitute Jewison Bennette scored, but time ran out for Tony Mowbray's side and Fulham went through to a 5th round tie against Leeds.

I left hoping that Tony Mowbray's team would win promotion as they and their vocal supporters would be an asset to the Premier League. But they didn't.

**Sunderland 2 (Clarke 77, Bennette 90) Fulham 3
(Wilson 8, Pereira 59, Kurawa 82)
Attendance 29,651**

69. Burton Albion v Exeter City

11 Febraury 2023 – Pirelli Stadium – League One

Next was a more prosaic Saturday afternoon fixture at League One Burton Albion, which is reachable in a day return via Birmingham. Burton is a pretty run down town, famous for its brewery industry, which gives Burton Albion their nickname. It was no surprise on my walk to the ground to see an off licence was called Booze City.

The Pirelli Stadium was built in 2005 on the site of the Pirelli UK Tyre Company Sports and Social Club. Pirelli donated the land to the club in exchange for naming rights. Burton have been in the Football League since 2009 and can claim Roy McFarland, Gary Rowett, Jimmy Floyd Hasselbaink and Nigel Clough among their managers. They play in a fetching yellow strip and were currently in the charge of a Tunisian, Noureddine Maamria. Exeter were ten places above Burton in the table, but the home side made a lot of the running, and were perhaps a bit unlucky not to be given a penalty for hand ball just before half time.

Exeter played more strongly in the second half, but it was the home team which snatched the win after 84 minutes. Substitute Sam Winnall seized on a misplaced shot and lashed the ball into the roof of the net.

It was Burton's third win in a row and took them three points clear of relegation. They subsequently finished the season 14th.

Burton Albion 1 (Winnall 84) Exeter City 0

Attendance 3,105

70. Colchester United v Walsall

14 February 2023 – JobServe Community
Stadium – League Two

Being in Essex, Colchester feels just the other side of London, but in reality it's a good two hour drive with Tuesday evening rush hour traffic to deal with on the way there.

Colchester United play at the JobServe Community Stadium, which replaced their old ground at Layer Road in 2008. It claims to be the biggest entertainment venue in Essex, and has hosted Elton John. Unusually, programmes are free with the price of admission.

The match was a goalless draw – the worst match I'd watched to date. I suppose it was unrealistic to expect more on a miserable Tuesday evening in February from two teams in mid table. The Colchester goalkeeper was forced into a smart save in the first minute, and this turned out to be the highlight of the game. The match wasn't improved by a referee who demonstrated no sign of urgency, and was endlessly delaying free kicks while he lectured the players about pushing, with the obligatory 'I'm watching you' pointing at his eyes gesture.

After 70 matches I needed a break, and the following morning I indulged myself by flying to New Zealand to get some sun and watch a couple of test matches.

Colchester United 0 Walsall 0
Attendance 2,577

71. Walsall v Barrow

4 March 2023 – Bescot Stadium – League Two

I had an excellent break in New Zealand, and was fortunate to see an epic test match at the attractive Basin Reserve in Wellington, which England lost by only one run.

The final leg of my challenge would involve 22 matches in just over 9 weeks. By coincidence my next match also involved Walsall so, refreshed by the break if somewhat jet-lagged, I took the Saturday morning train to the West Midlands.

The club has the fortune to have a station of the same name right opposite the Bescot Stadium, an out of town ground opened in 1990 by no less a celebrity than Sir Stanley Matthews. A fascinating aspect of English history is how different towns established pre-eminence in a niche market. In the case of Walsall their product was saddles, hence the club's nickname.

This was another fairly meaningless match between two mid-table teams but at least it had a goal. It was scored midway through the first half by Barrow forward Billy Waters, whose Wikipedia entry says is also a talented singer. There was an element of luck as a shot from the edge of the area was deflected into his path, but he finished well. This defeat ended Walsall's remarkable sequence of six consecutive draws, though not in the way they would have wanted.

I was also following events in the Premier League and was much cheered when Arsenal, who had a ten point lead over Manchester City, went two goals down to lowly Bournemouth. But they pulled two goals back and, while I was listening to the radio on Bescot Station, Reiss Nelson scored a dramatic winner for them in the 97th minute. At this point it seemed that the force was with them and that they would go on to win the League.

Walsall 0 Barrow 1 (Waters 22)
Attendance 5,018

72. Huddersfield Town v Bristol City

7 March 2023 – John Smith's Stadium – EFL Championship

Next was a Tuesday evening Championship match at Huddersfield. The only person I associate with Huddersfield is actually a Scotsman, Denis Law, who I watched after he moved to Manchester City in 1960 for what was then a record fee of £55,000. The fee paid for the installation of floodlights at their ground, which were known as the 'Denis Law Lights'. But the statue which greets you as you leave Huddersfield Station is of an authentic Yorkshireman, former Prime Minister Harold Wilson.

Huddersfield Town's ground was built in 1994 as the McAlpine Stadium, but is now called the John Smith's Stadium as it is sponsored by a company which makes a gassy drink which it markets as beer. The ground is owned by Kirklees Council and is also used by Huddersfield Giants Rugby League club.

Huddersfield have a proud pedigree having won both the First Division three times in a row and the FA Cup in the 1920s. More recently they had fallen into harder times but were now back in the Championship, and only missed promotion to the Premier League when they lost the 2022 playoff final to Nottingham Forest. But this season had gone badly and they were now bottom of the table. This called for desperate measures and they turned to an old hand, Neil Warnock, who had first managed them 30 years previously.

Fate decreed that I should watch yet another 0-0 draw. Huddersfield didn't manage a shot on target in the first half, and only did slightly better after half time. They came closest when Weimann cleared off the line for Bristol City at the death. But they won a point which took them off the bottom place. 'Remind me to bring my Sudoku next time' said the bloke behind me to his neighbour.

Subsequently Colin, to give Warnock his anagrammatically derived nickname, must have rediscovered some of his old managerial skills, because Huddersfield escaped relegation comfortably and finished in 17th place.

Huddersfield Town 0 Bristol City 0
Attendance 17,177

73. Crewe Alexandra v Salford City

10 March 2023 – Mornflake Stadium – League Two

Crewe wouldn't exist without its status as a railway junction, so this was an easy journey. Their Gresty Road ground, now operating as the Mornflake Stadium, is only a few minutes' walk from the station. Bizarrely, in 2015 it hosted an international friendly between Northern Ireland and Qatar, and one of its stands is called the Ice Cream Van Stand.

After one goal in three matches, I felt I was due some action, and was duly rewarded. Crewe Alexandra – 'The Alex' – were in the lower half of the table, and faced Salford who were lying seventh. The away side took an early lead with a neat goal after the wing had skinned the fullback, but Crewe had a chance to equalise when Salford conceded a penalty. Dan Agyei, who had originally come through the youth system at Wimbledon, has one of those stuttering run-ups which don't inspire confidence, but he buried the kick. Shortly before half time, Crewe took the lead when the 19 year old Joel Tabiner spotted the keeper off his line and cleverly lobbed him from 30 yards. But Salford struck back to equalise and it was 2-2 at the break.

The second half was open with some end-to-end play, but there were no goals till the 85th minute, when Salford scored what they must have thought was the winner. However Crewe equalised again with a neat back heel after a melee following a corner and then, amid growing excitement, Agyei seized on a rebound from the keeper and scored the winner in the 90th minute. There were still seven minutes of stoppage time, but despite attacks at both ends the match finished 4-3. An excellent match played in a clean spirit.

This spirit did not extend to the spectators. The Salford supporters must have been pretty disgruntled and there was some potential aggro outside the station after the match which resulted in a policeman feeling that he needed to escort me across the road between the two sets of spectators!

Salford's season was the subject of a Sky Sports series called 'The Class of 92' and this game featured, including a passionate expletive laden post-match dressing room rant about losing a two goal lead from manager Neil Wood. The documentary went on to show Salford squeaking into 7th place on the last day of the season, before losing the play-off on penalties to local rivals Stockport.

Crewe Alexandra 4 (Agyei 30p, 90 Tabiner 40, O'Riordan 88)
Salford City 3 (Barry 19, Hendry 45, Mallan 85)
Attendance 4,311

74. Preston North End v Cardiff City

11 March 2023 – Deepdale – EFL Championship

By train from Crewe to Preston where I met up with a friend who lived locally, though not that locally because it took him three attempts to find a pub which was still open. My long standing friend from university Julian, who has supported Preston from childhood, kindly procured me a ticket for this match.

Preston is a founder member of the Football League, and have played at their Deepdale ground ever since. They famously had a 100% record in their first season. The club's, and possibly the town's, most famous son, Sir Tom Finney, is commemorated with both a statue and a street named after him.

Preston harboured play-off ambitions, whereas Cardiff's league position was a bit lowly for comfort. The first half was lively but goalless. There were chances at both ends and it seemed certain a goal would come, it was just a matter of at which end. In fact it was Preston who scored. Striker Tom Cannon, on loan from Everton, dispossessed a defender and hit a clever finish into the top of the net. The main action came in the last minutes. A Cardiff defender sliced a clearance horribly; Cannon followed up, and was cleaned out by the Cardiff goalkeeper Alnwick, who was their second choice as their regular keeper had been sent off the previous week! Red card. There was a long delay while the third choice keeper got ready. He had a transient moment of glory when he saved the resulting free kick, but only parried the ball into the path of Preston substitute Ched Evans who made it 2-0.

I sat next to a delightful and interesting guy. He introduced himself as Ziggy, presumably short for Zbigniew or similar, as his father had fought in the Free Polish Division at Monte Cassino. A retired headmaster who was now the Discipline and Absenteeism Advisor to the Merseyside Education Department. Good luck with that Ziggy!

Preston North End 2 (Cannon 68, Evans 90+4) Cardiff City 0
Attendance 14,295

75. Cardiff City v West Bromwich Albion

15 March 2023 – Cardiff City Stadium – EFL Championship

The luck of the draw had me watching Cardiff twice in succession. The day before I had one of the most pleasurable evenings of my life, watching Manchester City beat RB Leipzig 7-0 in the Champions League second leg. Their goal machine Erling Haaland scored five of those between the 28th minute and being subbed off just after an hour.

The next morning I caught a leisurely stopping train to Cardiff, with Andy Townsend in my carriage as far as Crewe, and then spent the afternoon at Cardiff Castle – a magnificent attraction which, although dating back to Roman times, has a splendid house which was turned into an opulent Gothic home in the late 19th century by the Bute family – then the wealthiest in Britain. While there I learned my piece of trivia for the day – Cardiff was where the first million pound cheque was written, by the US Navy to the South Wales Coal Company in 1909.

The old Ninian Park (or Parc Ninian) was knocked down in 2009 and replaced by the boringly named Cardiff City Stadium which was built next door. The bars are literally cashless – you have to order from a machine on the opposite wall, and present your receipt at the bar.

Cardiff were lying 21st, perilously close to the drop zone, while West Brom were eighth, within a few points of the playoff spots. Since I had last watched them, they had dispensed with the services of Steve Bruce, and appointed a 21st century manager, the Spanish Carlos Corberan, who had previously managed Huddersfield and Olympiakos.

Another minute's silence before kick-off, this time for the four women who had died in a car accident which lay undiscovered for four days. West Brom took the lead after 17 minutes – a move started by the veteran Marc Albrighton, on loan from Leicester, and finished with a smart volley by the American Daryl Dike. They continued to look slightly the better side but couldn't convert a couple of chances to increase their lead. Midway through the second half, Cardiff's Guinea international Sory Kaba got his head to a cross. West Brom keeper Griffiths got his hand to the ball but it dribbled inside the post. The match ended 1-1, with Cardiff the happier of the two teams. And they had managed 90 minutes without having their goalkeeper sent off.

The following morning I had time for a brief visit to the Museum of Wales, and then travelled home by bus, thanks to yet another rail strike.

Cardiff City 1 (Kaba 65) WBA 1 (Dike 17)
Attendance 17,785

76. AFC Wimbledon v Crawley Town

18 March 2023 – Cherry Red Records Stadium – League Two

Wimbledon was the club I should have visited back in September but for the death of the Queen. I never watched the original Wimbledon at the old Plough Lane but a friend of mine once went as the guest of a director, and swears that he encountered vomit on the floor of the Directors' Box!

AFC Wimbledon was formed in the aftermath of the original club decanting to Milton Keynes. Their new stadium, built on the site of the Old Wimbledon Greyhound Stadium, had opened there just over two years previously, is sponsored as the Cherry Red Records Stadium. It goes a step further than the Cardiff Stadium in the automation stakes, with automated beer dispensers – you just tap your card and the machine pours you a pint.

AFC were 17th and Crawley occupied a relegation spot in 23rd. The most well-known player on display was AFC's Chris Gunter, who had won over 100 caps with Wales, being part of the squad which reached the Euro 2016 semi-finals. The match was pretty unmemorable. Crawley took an early lead with a close range tap in after six minutes and held on for the remaining 84. It was their first away win of the season which occasioned some joyful singing, and lifted them out of the relegation zone. From the home crowd there were more boos than songs.

I got home in time to watch Manchester City put six past Burnley in the FA Cup, and Haaland score yet another hat-trick, making eight goals in five days.

AFC Wimbledon 0, Crawley Town 1 (Nadesan 6)
Attendance 7,300

77. Exeter City v Accrington Stanley

25 March 2023 – St James Park – League One

The following Saturday brought a trip to the charming city of Exeter. It's a brisk uphill one mile walk, past a statue to Boer War General Sir Redvers Buller, from St David's Station to Exeter's town centre. I had time for a quick look inside the cathedral, and then to take a tour of the amazing underground passages, which were built in the 13ᵗʰ century to bring water from outside town to the cathedral. The tour is not for the claustrophobic or the very tall – my hard hat took several sturdy blows.

Exeter City, known as 'The Grecians' for a reason which isn't entirely clear, is owned by its supporters. In 1914 they toured Brazil and were the opponents in what is generally acknowledged to be the first match played by the Brazil national team. They have occupied their St James Park ground, adjacent to a railway station of the same name, since 1904. They were comfortable in mid table, while Accrington occupied a relegation spot in 21ˢᵗ place.

Exeter made most of the running in the first half, with Jay Stansfield prominent, but took 39 minutes to score. Demetri Mitchell, who had come through the Manchester United youth system, cut inside, made space for himself just outside the area and rifled the ball into the top of the net. Goals came more freely in the second half. First winger Josh Key beat the full back one on one, then Sam Nombe poked home a close range header after a shot struck the bar. Finally Jay Stansfield assisted the fourth goal and then scored the fifth himself.

The Accrington fans on the station afterwards were in a philosophical mood considering the lengthy journey home they faced. 'I'm insulating my kitchen floor,' said one 'To think instead I could have spent the day working on my back in the dark breathing insulation fibres.'

Exeter City 5 (Mitchell 36, Key 49, Nombe 54, Scott 75, Stansfield 81) Accrington Stanley 0
Attendance 6,556

78. Tranmere Rovers v Harrogate Town

31 March 2023 – Prenton Park – League One

The Wirral is mainly a beautiful part of Cheshire, but Birkenhead isn't the most salubrious area. It does however have the splendid Birkenhead Priory, almost 1000 years old, whose St Mary's Tower affords a magnificent view across the Mersey to Liverpool. The steps of the tower are dedicated as a memorial to the 99 people who died in the submarine SS Thetis, which tragically sank off the coast of Llandudno on its maiden dive in June 1939. I was at school with a lad called Howard Woods, whose father Lieutenant Woods was one of the four survivors. He sued the admiralty for damages after the inquiry attributed some of the blame to him, and the damages he won enabled him to send his son to private school. The really sad story is told in an excellent book called 'The Admiralty Regrets'

Prenton Park is an old established ground, much too big for a League Two team. The away supporters are accommodated at one end in an area called the Cowshed Stand.

Local celebrity and national treasure Paul O'Grady had died three days earlier, but the club chose not to commemorate this.

Crawley Town, who were just above the relegation zone, took an early lead through their striker Luke Armstrong, who tied his blonde hair in a ponytail, Erling Haaland style. A few minutes later, he had another good chance, but, unlike his Norwegian doppelganger, took a touch and the opportunity went begging.

After 36 minutes Tranmere won a free kick about 35 yards out. It looked too far out for a shot, but Hughes took the chance. His shot hit the post and cannoned in off the unfortunate keeper. Armstrong missed a good one on one chance in the second half, and Tranmere had a couple of good opportunities for a late winner, but a draw was probably a fair result.

Up the road, there was live music at the Sportsman's Arms, which was selling Doom Bar at £2.50 a pint, and whose clientele had an average Body Mass Index of about 30. It was someone's 60th birthday and a good time was had by all.

Tranmere Rovers 1 (Oxley og 36) Harrogate Town 1 (Armstrong 4) Attendance 5,861

79. Everton v Tottenham Hotspur

3 April 2023 – Goodison Park – Premier League

Up north again for the Monday night match. Before the game, in the local Wetherspoons, the Thomas Frost, an Everton fan took great pleasure in showing me drone shots on his phone of the impressive new stadium going up. Goodison Park is in its last seasons, and inevitably has a slightly tired appearance. However, the atmosphere was brilliant, as this was a big match for both teams with Spurs lying 4th and Everton, who had replaced Frank Lampard with Sean Dyche a few weeks previously, 18th. The first half was nondescript, the only events of note being a drinks break at 26 minutes to allow Ramadan observers to take on fluids at sunset, and Kane putting a header wide from about 10 yards.

But the match sprang into life on the hour. Kane fouled Gray and had an altercation with Doucoure, who put his hand in his face. It was a clear red card, though Kane adopted the irritating practice of making an unnecessary meal of it. Shortly after Keane conceded a penalty and Kane sent his England team mate Jordan Pickford the wrong way. This looked enough to get the points but Lucas Moura, having only been on for a few minutes, levelled the red card count with a bad challenge. And, with stoppage time beckoning, Michael Keane hit a screamer into the top corner from 25 yards – think Vincent Kompany's late winner, Manchester City v Leicester 2019, which prompted

Gary Nevill to ask 'where do you want your statue Vinny?' An important and deserved point for Everton, who eventually finished 27th, escaping relegation by two points.

Everton 1 (Keane 90) Spurs 1 (Kane pen 68)
Attendance 39,294

80. Accrington Stanley v Port Vale

9 April 2023 – Wham Stadium – League One

Easter weekend and three matches to watch. The Good Friday drive up to Accrington took 5½ hours against a forecast of under four. The first really warm day of spring contributed to a friendly and welcoming atmosphere at the Wham Stadium, which scores good marks for having a real ale outlet selling the splendidly named Accy Ale.

Port Vale were reasonably safely placed, but Accrington were 21st in the table. The match was uneventful for the first half hour. Then Accrington launched a hopeful high ball into the Port Vale goalmouth. It was dropping just on the line, but the goalkeeper managed to fumble it into the net. Accrington doubled their lead just before half time, with a more orthodox goal scoring from about six yards from a pullback. Their third goal came from a second half penalty. Many of the 1100 Port Vale supporters, who comprised one third of the crowd, left at this point and they missed the final indignity when Funso Ojo, who had conceded the penalty, was sent off after a fairly pointless mass brawl just near the end. It was Accrington's biggest win of the season.

On returning to the Castle Inn where I was staying, I ordered a beer. When I had checked in earlier then owner John had asked me the purpose of my visit, and I had explained. On returning to the bar he put down my pint and £50. 'A donation to your charity'. An unexpected act of generosity...

In the evening I watched the televised late kick-off match, Middlesbrough v Burnley. Burnley won 2-1 to clinch promotion to the Premier League prompting big celebrations for Vincent Kompany and his team. When I returned to the Castle Inn I found many of its customers were the worse for wear having been celebrating too. Those of my age explained that their excuse for supporting Burnley was that when they were growing up it was their nearest league club as Accrington Stanley had gone out of business.

The following morning before driving to Wolverhampton I saw the moving memorial to the Accrington Pals Battalion, probably the best known of these Great War volunteer battalions. 720 men from this unit took part in the opening day of the Somme offensive. 584 of these were killed, wounded or missing.

**Accrington Stanley 3 (Stevens og 31, Rodgers 40,
Pressley 68 p)   Port Vale 0
Attendance 3,444**

81. Wolverhampton Wanderers v Chelsea

10 April 2023 – Molineux – Premier League

Easter Saturday was another nice spring day, and this was a big match for both teams. My friend John had kindly enabled me to procure a ticket. Molyneux, or 'The Molyneux' as fans rather pretentiously call it, has a slightly odd design, with a stand in the corner at the far end facing the side stand rather than the pitch.

Wolves were not clear of the threat of relegation, and Chelsea, seriously underperforming in 11th place, had just reappointed Frank Lampard as temporary manager to replace the sacked Graham Potter.

Chelsea did nothing to disprove their league position, and Wolves were quicker to the ball and more adventurous throughout. Their keeper Sa played in a fetching lilac outfit, the colour of the sort of sickly soft drinks which are sold in hot third world countries. He looked disconcertingly like a young Jimmy Savile. The match was settled by a spectacular goal by Matheus Nunes on the half hour. He was right in front of me, on the right hand corner of the penalty area, when a corner was recycled and then headed clear. Nobody moved to close him down, so he had an age to set himself and, as the ball dropped, he hit a perfect volley past Kepa into the top corner. It was his first goal for Wolves, and turned out to be his only one, as he was bought by Manchester City in the summer.

For some reason the electronic scoreboard never displayed the team names, and with the PA pretty unintelligible, one had to work out the teams by looking up their numbers on the programme. Obviously many were well known to me, for example Diego Costa who must have a career ahead after football as a baddy in a Western. But it came as quite a shock to me, when Lampard made a substitution, to see that the player going off was Raheem Sterling. He'd played for an hour and I'd never even noticed him. Lampard brought on Mount and Aubamayang, but Chelsea made little impression and Wolves earned three valuable points.

There was a historic post-script to this match. Several months later Wolves became the first club to be fined for homophobic chanting. This cost them £100,000.

Wolves 1 (Nunes 31) Chelsea 0
Attendance 31,614

82. Barrow v Crawley Town

10 April 2023 – SO Legal Stadium – League Two

I had Easter Sunday spare before my next match at Barrow, so I went for a longish walk in the Forest of Bowland and then stayed in the historic city of Lancaster. Driving north the following day I spent an hour at the impressive ruins of Furness Abbey, founded by King Stephen.

Before automatic promotion/relegation to the Conference was introduced, the bottom club in the bottom tier had to apply for re-election. In 1972 Barrow became the first club to fall foul of this process, when they were defeated by Hereford who had scored a famous FA Cup victory against Newcastle that season. Their most famous football export was Emlyn Hughes, who is commemorated with a statue just outside the hotel where I stayed. Barrow spent the following 48 years in various levels of non-league football, and had several brushes with insolvency. In 2020 they returned to the football league, being promoted on the basis of points per match as the season was curtailed by the Covid pandemic.

Their ground, which goes by the name of the SO Legal Stadium, is very much like a non league ground, and I was told the club would have to add 1,000 seats in the summer to bring it up to league standard.

Barrow were in mid table, their opponents Crawley Town in relegation trouble. Barrow opened the scoring with a far post tap in by Josh Gordon after 18 minutes, and then had another effort disallowed for handball. Gordon, who hailed from Stoke and had spent three seasons with Walsall, added another after half time following a long throw, and completed a hat-trick from the penalty spot ten minutes later, although the keeper got a hand to his shot. They completed the rout with a header near the end by Gerard Garner, which pleased my neighbour who said he was their record signing and it was his first goal for the club. I couldn't find out what he had cost, but he had come from Fleetwood and Barrow's previous record was just £20,000.

Barrow is the most remote club in the football league and their players come from far and wide. I suggested to my neighbour that getting together for training must be an issue. 'Not really' he said 'they train in Manchester'.

In the evening I refuelled in the local Wetherspoons, the Furness Railway. A few weeks later this establishment made headlines when one of its customers left some secret papers in the gents. These contained design details of a nuclear submarine under construction at the massive BAe Systems facility which provides most of the local employment.

Barrow 4 (Gordon 18, 47, 56p, Garner 81) Crawley Town 0
Attendance 3,345

83. Middlesbrough v Norwich City

14 April 2023 – Riverside Stadium – EFL Championship

In 2011 my friend Chris and I did the coast-to-coast walk across the north of England – just under 200 miles in 14 days. I can still remember the excitement at about the halfway point, when we had our first glimpse of the east coast. The view then was dominated by the massive industrial complex of Redcar/Middlesbrough/Stockton. Much has since closed, giving the city quite a feeling of deprivation. On arriving at Middlesbrough station, I was greeted by a poster from the Cleveland Fire Service saying 'Let's Stamp out Arson' – a sad commentary on the social priorities in the town.

The Riverside Stadium was built in the mid-1990s to replace the old Ayresome Park. To open it, Middlesbrough played a pre-season friendly against an Italian side, and the away players complained about the dressing room facilities – no hair dryers! It is well appointed, though didn't look its best in the pouring rain.

This was a big promotion match, with 'Boro lying third and Norwich only a point out of the play-off spots. Conditions were filthy – standing water in many parts of the pitch, and if the rain had got any heavier abandonment would have been on the cards. Middlesbrough took an early lead when a cross was turned in at the far post by Ramsey and increased their lead after 42 minutes – a slightly controversial goal as Norwich had their left back down injured. Sensing a lengthy delay for the goal celebration and injury, I made an early getaway for a half time toilet break. Amazingly, as I stood on the concourse I watched on TV as no less than three more goals were scored – a third for 'Boro, one for Norwich and a fourth for the home team after 6 minutes of stoppage time. The match was therefore over as a contest, but Middlesbrough added a fifth through Chuba Akpom, who had spent his early years at Arsenal. Both teams continued to play remarkably good football, despite the dreadful conditions. Middlesbrough goalkeeper, USA international Zak Steffen, wasn't unduly troubled. After three years at Manchester City as number two to Ederson, he'd chosen to go out on loan so as to get game time ahead of the Qatar World Cup but it didn't work out for him, as he wasn't selected.

Middlesbrough 5 (Ramsey 7, Hackney 41, Archer 43, 45+6, Akpom 49) Norwich City 1 (Sargent 45) Attendance 26,429

84. Rotherham v Luton Town

15 Apeil 2023 – AESSEAL New York Stadium –
EFL Championship

From Middlesbrough via a change at York to Rotherham – a town with no discernible tourist attractions. Rotherham United's stadium has to have the silliest name in the football league. The sponsors with a name you can't even pronounce make seals, and the 'New York' part apparently derives from the fact that a foundry called Guest and Chrimes on the site used to make fire hydrants for the city of New York. The stadium was built in 2012, replacing the old Millmoor ground.

Since I had watched them in August, Luton had had their manager Nathan Jones recruited by Southampton, and then sacked a few weeks later. To replace Jones they had hired Rob Edwards, who himself had been victim of the Watford hire and fire merry-go-round.

Edwards had clearly done a good job, taking Luton to 4th place, and the visitors brought over 3000 noisy fans. The first half was uneventful apart from a remarkable save by the Rotherham goalkeeper, before Luton Striker Carlton Morris received a through pass, cut inside his marker, and scored with a strong shot into the top of the net to put his team in front. A few minutes into the second half, a Rotherham defender clumsily handled a cross in the area. Cauley Woodrow's penalty was saved, but he was able to tap in the rebound. The last forty minutes were fairly uneventful and Luton ran out 2-0 winners.

The Millers had oscillated between the second and third tiers for five consecutive season, but eventually achieved safety from relegation with a match to spare. Luton got into the play-offs, threatening the Premier League with its scruffiest stadium.

**Rotherham United 0, Luton Town 2 (Morris 45
Woodrow 47)
Attendance 11,009**

85. Blackpool v West Bromwich Albion

18 April 2023 – Broomfield Road Stadium– EFL Championship

To Blackpool by train with a spare afternoon to enjoy before this Tuesday evening fixture. It was a lovely spring day and the promenade looked splendid, even if it was too early in the season for the attractions to be open. The venerable Bloomfield Road Stadium is over 120 years old. I expected there would be a statue to Stanley Mathews, but the club has chosen to honour the equally legendary Jimmy Armfield.

Blackpool were flirting with relegation, while their opponents harboured play-off ambitions. They should have taken an early lead but Morgan Rogers (yet another Manchester City loan player) hit the post from a good position. West Brom scored first after some slack marking at a corner, but Blackpool still made a few chances. Albion sealed the game on the hour after some casual defending by Blackpool.

The result allowed West Bromwich to climb five places to sixth and left Blackpool 23rd.

I then embarked on a crazy journey in my desire to follow Manchester City's pursuit of the Champions League. A late train to Manchester which just missed the last connection to Manchester Airport.

An uncomfortable couple of hours on the station before

getting to Ringway Airport for a crack of dawn flight to Dusseldorf and catching a train to Munich.

**Blackpool 0, WBA 2 (Thomas-Asante 18,
Gardner-Hickman 60)
Attendance 10,705**

86. Bolton Wanderers v Shrewsbury Town

22 April 2023 – University of Bolton Stadium – League One

Another train trip to Lancashire. My great grandfather William Lee was born in the Burnden district of Bolton, and I'd been to Bolton's old Burnden Park ground in my youth. In 1997 the club built a new stadium, the Reebok, and this, now named the University of Bolton Stadium, is served by Horwich Parkway station. At the front is a statue commemorating the club's most famous son, Nat Lofthouse.

It was almost exactly 50 years since the famous 'Stanley Mathews final' in which Blackpool beat Bolton 4-3, but many Bolton fans wore shirts to commemorate a more recent, though less glamorous, trip to Wembley – they had beaten Plymouth in the Papa Johns Cup Final three weeks earlier.

Bolton were in 7th place, Shrewsbury mid table and the match reflected these placings. After a scoreless 45 minutes, at half time by the wonders of technology, I was able to watch some cricket. My son Adam was playing in a preseason friendly at a club which had a streaming facility, so I watched him bat for a few minutes. (The few minutes was the length of half time, his innings lasted a bit longer!). In the second half Bolton broke the deadlock when Welsh international midfielder Josh Sheehan scored with a fine left foot shot from 20 yards.

This proved the match winner which enabled Bolton to climb into 5th place. Before my return train I had time to watch the first half of Manchester City's FA Cup semi-final against Sheffield United which they negotiated safely.

Bolton W 1 (Sheehan 63) Shrewsbury Town 0
Attendance 18,596

87. Grimsby Town v Crewe Alexandra

22 April 2023 – Blundell Road – League Two

Three months after my trip to Grimsby had been aborted due to a frozen pitch, I returned for a midweek fixture against Crewe. On my previous visit I'd spent the afternoon in the Fishing Heritage Centre, where I had the good luck to be shown round by a really interesting retired trawler skipper who had spent over 50 years at sea. The centre was really well laid out and gave an excellent impression of how cold, cramped and wet conditions at sea used to be. I had always assumed that the decline in our East Coast fishing industry was due to joining the EU and having all those dastardly foreigners sharing our fish. But my guide said that the real downturn started when Iceland imposed a 200 mile territorial limit. Grimsby has struggled to replace that industry and has all the hallmarks of a deprived town – Poundland, betting shops, tanning salons.

As any football anorak knows, the 19th century Blundell Park ground isn't actually in Grimsby. It's in Cleethorpes, one stop on the train from Grimsby, followed by a bracing walk along the front of this faded seaside resort.

There wasn't much riding on this end of season match between two mid table sides. Grimsby took an early lead when a neat free kick routine caught the Crewe defence unawares. Instead of crossing into the area, the ball was passed down the right wing to give Irish midfielder Holohan a clear chance. Crewe's Daniel Agyei went close a couple times before Danilo Orsi sealed the three points with a neat glancing header.

The match finished after the last train, but I was able to walk back to Grimsby and complete my 10,000 steps before closing time.

Grimsby Town 2 (Holohan 13, Orsi-Dadomo 82)
Crewe Alexandra 0
Attendance 4,482

88. Chelsea v Brentford

26 April 2023 – Stamford Bridge – Premier League

I was lucky enough to get into Stamford Bridge using the season ticket of my friend Dan, who was away. To collect the ticket, I met up at the Peter Osgood statue with his father Andy, a well-known broadcaster and lifelong Chelsea fan. Andy was very grumpy about Chelsea's form, saying he couldn't see where their next goal was coming from, let alone the next point. He was particularly scathing about Lampard's management ability and about Sterling and Havertz. I think he would have skipped the game had he not needed to give me Dan's season ticket.

Andy's analysis wasn't far wrong, and he opted to leave at half time, by which time Brentford had taken the lead with an own goal from Azpilicueta. Chelsea's abundance of riches was apparent – their squad size exceeded the number of lockers in the changing room – when they brought on Aubameyang and Mudryk for the second half. The mood among the other season ticket holders was also pretty mutinous and dozens left when Mbeumo added a second 12 minutes from time. A solid all round performance by Brentford, and Lampard's fifth consecutive defeat since taking over from the sacked Graham Potter.

I was less than totally gripped by the match as I had one ear tuned to the radio following Manchester City v Arsenal, where City achieved an excellent 4-1 win to put the team firmly in the driving seat for the Premier League.

Chelsea 0 Brentford 2 (Azpilicueta og 37, Mbeumo 78)
Attendance 39,929

89. Tottenham Hotspur v Manchester United

27 April 2023 – Tottenham Hotspur Stadium – Premier League

The following night I again had the good fortune to have the use of a season ticket, this time at Spurs for the visit of Manchester United.

Their new stadium is a bit of a pain to get to by public transport, but is now probably the best appointed in the Premier League. There was warm applause as the stadium announcer was able to say 'and a big welcome back to Christian Eriksen'. 'Harry Kane, we'll see you in June' sang the United fans, optimistically as it turned out.

This was a huge match, with the fourth Champions League spot potentially at stake. Spurs, who were on the back of a 6-1 thrashing at Newcastle, started poorly, and fell behind after 7 minutes when Sancho was given enough room to fire a powerful shot across Frazer Forster, who was standing in for the injured Lloris. They avoided another when Peresic headed off the line, but conceded a second just before the break. A long ball found Rashford, who held off Dier and scored emphatically with his left foot. 'Get out of our club' sang the Spurs fans to Daniel Levy, before booing their team off at the break.

The match came to life after half time. Tottenham upped their game and soon pulled a goal back. Kane's shot was blocked but Porro skilfully steered the rebound home with the outside of his foot. Bruno Fernandes hit the bar when he'd broken clear on goal, before Dier headed wide when it was easier to score than to miss. Anthony Taylor illustrated the adage that it's much harder to get a second yellow card than the first, by only awarding a free kick when Lindelof cynically hacked down Son. Finally Tottenham earned a draw when Kane played in Son for a characteristic far post finish.

An excellent match and a fair result.

Tottenham Hotspur 2 (Porro 56, Son 79)
Manchester United 2 (Sancho 7, Rashford 44)
Attendance 61,586

90. Morecambe FC v Lincoln City

29 April 2023 – Mazuma Stadium/Globe Arena – League One

The Globe Arena was built in 2010 and is a pleasant lower division stadium, with terracing along one side. In the corner is a gym owned by, and named after, local resident Tyson Fury.

This was a relegation thriller. Lincoln were in mid table but Morecambe were lying 21st, two points below MK Dons and Oxford United. Their battle for survival got off to a bad start when, after a bout of head tennis, the ball fell to Lincoln's Danish midfielder Sorensen who scored with a well-placed shot. Morecambe hit the post soon after, but shortly after half time Lincoln scored a second through Matty Virtue, whose full name according to Wikipedia is Matthew Joseph Virtue-Thick. I think I'd stick to a single barrelled name if I'd been given that handle.

At this point Morecambe were effectively relegated, as MK Dons were leading Barnsley 4-1. They got a goal back within two minutes and then, after much pressure, equalised when their striker Stockton out jumped the keeper. At the same time, news was coming through that Barnsley were pulling goals back at MK Dons. The woodwork was hit at both ends before, amid mounting excitement, Stockton headed home from a free kick, and the crowd heard that Barnsley had equalised. There were eight minutes of stoppage time and Morecambe held on for a famous win before a stadium record crowd.

They were still alive, though they would have to do better than MK Dons in the final match the following weekend.

I had a pleasant walk along the front of another out of season Lancashire resort before the train home. This was my final rail journey and Avanti West Coast had the last word by cancelling my train from Lancaster and causing me yet another late arrival.

Morecambe FC 3 (Stockton 50, 86, Niasse 66)
Lincoln City 2 (Sorenson 30, Virtue 49)
Attendance 5,769

91. Fleetwood Town v Ipswich Town

7 May 2023 – Highbury Stadium – League One

For a few hours, Project All 92 was threatened with becoming Project 91. Twelve days before the match I had an email from Fleetwood saying that the police were asking for strict check of home fans and, as I had no previous purchase record with the club, my ticket was cancelled without a refund. I replied saying that I was not an away fan, explaining my project, and arguing that at the age of 78 I didn't really fit the profile of a hooligan. Luckily for me there was an outbreak of common sense, and my ticket was reinstated.

This was the final round of League One matches, the day after the coronation. Plymouth and Ipswich had already secured automatic promotion, but with Plymouth one point ahead, the championship still had to be decided. And as a sub-plot, Ipswich were on 99 goals for the season. The first half was fairly uneventful, but Ipswich took the lead early in the second half with a fierce close range shot from Freddie Ladapo into the roof of the net from a narrow angle. This was their first century of goals since Alf Ramsey took them to the league title in 1961. A win wouldn't give them the League One championship though, as Plymouth were winning at Port Vale. Fleetwood got on level terms a few minutes later, when Marriott seized on a loose ball, and he gave them the lead with a glancing header in the 71st minute, before Ipswich equalised a few minutes later. The last meaningful action occurred when Ipswich's Harry Clarke earned a day off for their opening match in the Championship next season by getting sent off for a second yellow card.

They weren't champions but Ipswich fans could at least still sing 'The Town are going up'.

Meanwhile Morecambe failed to profit from their reprieve of the previous weekend and were relegated after losing 3-2 at Exeter, joining Accrington and MK Dons. Cambridge escaped the drop with a win against Forest Green Rovers, who had been relegated long ago.

This was my third visit to the Northwest Lancashire coast in a month. Fleetwood, once the third largest fishing port in the country, is now a sleepy seaside town, whose most famous product is Fisherman's Friend cough sweets, a family business founded in 1865. I parked outside a tattoo parlour humorously called 'Gentle Prick' and had a pleasant walk along the front in spring sunshine to Rossall Point, where there is an odd shaped observation tower. Then a scenic drive across the Pennines and down Nidderdale to the venue of my final match the next day.

Fleetwood Town 2 (Marriott 57, 69)
Ipswich Town 2 (Lapado 50, Harness 73)
Attendance 4,979

92. Harrogate Town v Rochdale

8 May 2023 – EnviroVent Stadium – League Two

My previous seven visits to Yorkshire had been to industrial cities or towns. Harrogate is different – a gentle spa town at the foot of the Yorkshire Dales.

Harrogate FC were only promoted to the Football League in 2020, and had to pay their first few home games at Doncaster while they replaced the artificial pitch with grass. The EnviroVent Stadium, another silly sponsored name, is much what you'd expect in the lower reaches of League Two – functional and friendly.

The main relevance of the match was that it was Rochdale's final appearance in the Football League, as they had been relegated after a record 102 years in the third and fourth tiers. As on the previous day the national anthem was played to mark the coronation.

Several hundred Rochdale spectators had made the trip for a valedictory match and they had reason to cheer after 24 minutes when their Irish midfielder Keohane scored after a good move. They exhibited fine gallows humour by singing 'One nil to the National League!' General opinion around me was that Harrogate would need a significant rebuild in the close season to stay up next year. Rochdale's lead lasted till the 74th minute, when Harrogate fullback Toby Sims side-footed a neat finish from the right. As a final gesture Harrogate brought on their veteran Northern Ireland defender Rory McCardle, who was retiring. The ref, who was also retiring, ran over and gave him a hug, and the match finished in an end of term atmosphere, with players and families staying on the pitch after the final whistle.

Harrogate Town 1 (Sims 74) Rochdale 1 (Keohane 24)
Attendance 3,234

Mission Accomplished

So that was it! All 92 grounds visited in just over 9 months – 283 days to be exact. (Apparently the record is 189 days). During this time there had been two monarchs and three prime ministers. For the statistically minded the matches comprised 36 home wins, 29 away wins and 27 draws, with 252 goals, just over 2.5 per match. Seven goalless draws, a couple of 4-3s and a 5-2. 72 League matches, 10 FA Cup ties, 7 Carabao Cup, 2 Europa League, and one Champions League group match. I saw Erling Haaland's first goal for Manchester City, and Cristiano Ronaldo's last for United. I had a first glimpse of the exciting talent of Manchester United's Alejandro Garnacho and, at the other end of the age spectrum, saw Dean Lewington's 735th match for MK Dons. I saw the key League One match at which Plymouth launched their bid for promotion by beating Ipswich, and was at the match which ended Steven Gerrard's reign at Aston Villa, ushering in the Unai Emery era. I watched Rochdale's last appearance in the Football League after 102 years. I was able to see some old favourites in the dugout, such as Joey Barton, Steve Bruce, Nigel Clough, Neil Warnock, and Kolo Toure, whose managerial stint only lasted 9 matches. Attendances varied from over 74,000 at Old Trafford to 1,059 at Salford City. As a valuable by-product, I got to know more of England by visiting many new places and sights, including Kenilworth Castle, Bowness Priory and the fine Royal Naval Museum in Hartlepool. And I was able to find where some of my ancestors were born or lived in Blackburn, Burnley, Carlisle and Rochdale.

The project formed as large part of my life, especially from January onwards. I budgeted to spend an average of £100 per match, but managed a bit less. I spent just under £3000 on hotel accommodation, and £1500 on train fares, greatly helped by my Senior Rail Card. My ticket costs, also sometimes reduced on account of my antiquity, averaged £22, and ranged from £97 (through a secondary ticket site) at Old Trafford to a ridiculously low £5 for FA Cup replays at Sunderland and Stockport.

From the start of the year I passed through Euston or King's Cross almost every week. Travelling by rail was a mixed experience. In general the north/south links are pretty good, but travelling east/west e.g. across the Pennines is slow. Arriva was probably the least reliable company and LNER one of the best. The latter is in public ownership – make of that what you will.

A few highlights:

Best match: The best quality match was the 2-2 draw in April between Spurs and Manchester United. The Manchester City v Borussia Dortmund Champions League match was pretty good too. The most exciting was Birmingham City's 4-3 win at Swansea, the experience being enhanced by being in the away section. Crewe v Salford also had an exciting ending.

Worst match: A few contenders here, but the 'winner' was the 0-0 draw between Colchester and Walsall, played on a freezing February evening between two mid table teams officiated by a referee who seemed determined to get involved and slow the game down even further.

Best goal: The best league goal was back in match 3 – Ismaila Sarr's astonishing 55 yarder for Watford at West Brom. Outside the league it was Erling Haaland's athletic kung fu strike against

Borussia Dortmund. Matheus Nunes technically perfect volley for Wolves against Chelsea was a close third.

Worst goal: I won't embarrass him by naming the Port Vale goalkeeper who claimed this award by dropping a perfectly harmless cross into his own net at Accrington.

Most exciting newcomer: Manchester United's Alejandro Garnacho

Best stadium: The Tottenham Hotspur Stadium is the newest and best appointed ground.

Best atmosphere: St James Park, with a special mention for the nearby Strawberry pub. In the lower divisions, the most welcoming was Accrington's Wham Stadium.

Best away fans: Borussia Dortmund supporters were amazing. Most vociferous English fans – West Ham.

Worst stadium: A close contest between Port Vale and Luton, though the latter will be given a bit of makeover to be fit for the Premier League. Most gormless stewards – Gillingham.

Food: My best half time grub was a £3 sausage and chips at Salford; my worst were pies of indeterminate provenance at Stockport and Wycombe, the latter costing £7.

Beer: Biggest rip-off £7.30 for a pint of lager outside the London Stadium. An unexpected bargain – Madri for £3 a pint at Old Trafford. The Glazers are missing a trick there.

Best programme: This has to go to Rochdale, who put out a commemorative issue marking the Queen's death 10 days after the event. I'd hoped to collect a full set of 92, but 10 clubs either no longer have print programmes, or make them too difficult to buy.

Accommodation:
I stayed in a hotels and pubs of varying quality. I have already given a shout out to John, the landlord of the Castle Inn in Accrington. Thanks again John.

Diversity: Must do better. Only a handful of BAME officials, and just four female referee's assistants.

Post Season

That was the end of my project, but the league season still had three weeks to run. As I drove back down the M1 from Harrogate, the final round of Championship matches were being played. Millwall were in sixth place at the kick-off and looked set for a playoff when they lead Blackburn 3-1, but they blew the lead and lost 4-3, allowing Sunderland to sneak into the fourth play-off spot, joining Luton, Middlesbrough and Coventry. A tasty all north east final seemed in prospect, but in the play-off semi-finals Sunderland lost to Luton, and Coventry beat Middlesbrough to ensure that an unfashionable club would be promoted to the Premier League.

In the Premier League wins for Nottingham Forest and Everton pointed to Leicester and Leeds joining Southampton in being relegated.

At a slightly lower level, the following evening saw the greatest comeback in play-off history. Sheffield Wednesday, having lost the first leg at Peterborough 4-0, won at home by the same score. After a goal each in extra time, Wednesday went through on penalties. The next day Barnsley beat Bolton Wanderers to set up a Yorkshire derby at Wembley. In the League Two playoffs Stockport County beat Salford City on penalties and Carlisle overcame Bradford to set up another all northern play-off final.

Meanwhile, in the Premier League Arsenal had suffered a dramatic fall off in results, and a defeat at Brighton meant that Manchester City only needed three points from their last three matches, and were hoping to clinch the title by beating Chelsea in their last home match on the penultimate Sunday of the season. But on the Saturday evening Arsenal lost 1-0 at Nottingham Forest – a result which ensured safety for Forest, and made City champions without kicking a ball. This enabled Guardiola to make nine changes for the Chelsea match, but they still won 1-0 before players and fans enjoyed the trophy presentation on a lovely early summer afternoon.

On the Monday evening there were more joyful scenes, this time at St James Park, where Newcastle celebrated securing a Champions League spot with a 0-0 draw against Leicester. The following night Brighton and Manchester City's 1-1 draw confirmed Brighton would play in the Europa League net season.

So the main issues to be decided on the last Sunday round of matches were the last two relegation spots, and the Europa Conference place for the 7th placed team.

The outcome was that Leeds and Leicester were relegated with Southampton, while Aston Villa beat Brighton to finished 7th and claim a place in the Europa Conference. And Brentford completed a double over Manchester City, who doubtless had an eye on their upcoming cup finals.

In the play-off finals, Carlisle beat Stockport on penalties to win promotion to win promotion to League One, and Luton defeated Coventry in the same way. Their reward of promotion to the Premier League is apparently worth £150 million, but the first £10 million had to be spent to make their ground adequate. The League One play-off final was also heading for penalties until deep into stoppage time in extra time, when Josh Windass headed a dramatic winner for Sheffield Wednesday against Barnsley, replicating his father Dean's feat for Hull City fifteen years earlier.

Now only two matches remained between Manchester City and the treble. I was abroad for the FA Cup Final – I'd booked to go on a tour with historian Dan Snow of the D Day beaches in Normandy. So on the Saturday evening, I was listening to our excellent guide with one ear, as our bus headed towards Omaha Beach, and my other ear was tuned to the commentary from the City website as the first all Manchester final kicked off. Reception was patchy, and my feed cut out for a few seconds. When it recovered I could only hear enormous cheering. A beep on my phone told me the good news – Gundogan had scored in 13 seconds! The match ended 2-1, and now only the Champions league final remained.

The Quest for the Champions League

Since the arrival of Pep Guardiola in 2017, Manchester City had found six different ways to get knocked out of the Champions League.

In his first season we won a splendid victory 5-3 against a Monaco team containing Kylian Mbappe and Bernardo Silva, but naively lost the away leg 3-1 and went out on away goals.

In 2018 City were victim of a 3 goal blitz at Anfield after spectators had thrown firecrackers at the team coach. City got an early goal in the return leg, and would have had a second before half time had VAR been in use then, but the deficit was too big to overcome.

The following year was against Spurs. The first leg was at the newly opened stadium and Spurs won 1-0 after Aguerro had missed a penalty. The return was a ding dong battle. After a mad 21 minutes City lead 3-2, and extended their lead to 4-2. But Spurs pulled it back to 4-3, which put them through on away goals. Llorente's final goal would have been disallowed had the hand ball rule which was introduced the following year been in force. In stoppage time Sterling had the ball in the net. The stadium erupted with Guardiola racing ecstatically down the touchline. But my joy only lasted a nanosecond, as I could see the referee holding his hand to his earpiece. VAR. Offside. Cruel beyond measure!

2020 was Covid year. In February, I was lucky enough to get a ticket to the Bernabeu for the away leg in the round of 16 against Real Madrid. Manchester City earned an exciting 2-1 win with two late goals, and I was delighted to meet up afterwards with my son Tim, who was working at the match. Then came lockdown, and the competition wasn't able to continue till August. We successfully navigated the return leg and then, meeting Olympic Lyonnais in the quarter final in a one leg match in Lisbon, played poorly and went out after Sterling had missed an open goal with five minutes remaining.

Then in 2021, City finally made the final, overcoming Borussia Dortmund and PSG en route. The match was in Porto, with many Covid restrictions still in place, and their opponents were Chelsea. Surely now our hour had arrived. I was so confident that I travelled up to Manchester to be take part in whatever celebrations must surely follow. I arrived to find all city centre pubs sold out, but managed to find a perch in a corner. The afternoon started well with Brentford winning their play-off final and gaining promotion to the Premier League. But the word 'anti-climax' doesn't even begin to describe what followed. Guardiola over thought his selection, playing without a holding mid-fielder. City played well below their best, not helped by Rudiger wiping out Kevin de Bruyne and fracturing his eye socket, and Chelsea won by a single goal.

The disappointment of 2022 was, if anything, worse. A tense quarterfinal against Atletico Madrid was won by a single goal in the home leg, scored by de Bruyne from Foden's pass. The return at the recently rebuilt Metropolitano Stadium was tense and brutal, and City held on for the most exciting 0-0 draw I've ever seen, with the second half lasting 57 minutes after an unseemly brawl. Agaun, I wss delighted to meet up with afterwards with Tim and his cameraman Andy White.

The semi-final draw brought the other Madrid team. In the home leg City went 2-0 up in 11 minutes, and subsequently lead 3-1 and 4-2. They should have put the tie to bed but the final score of 4-3 left the door open. The second leg at the Bernabeu was equally tense but a Mahrez goal put City two up on aggregate. As 90 minutes approached, I confess being on my phone checking the prices of Eurostar to Paris for the final. Then disaster struck – Rodrygo scored not once, but twice in a minute, and suddenly there was extra time. Shell-shocked, City conceded a third and went out. It felt like the ultimate choke.

Finally!

This year wa surely a case of now or never. City comfortably navigated the group stages and the round of 16, thrashing RB Leipzig 7-0 in the home leg. This brought Bayern Munich in the quarterfinal, and two late goals brought a good 3-0 win at the Etihad. I had a convoluted journey from Blackpool to Munich. It was worth the effort though, as the team, hanging onto a 3-0 lead, held Bayern off for an hour before Haaland scored to settle the tie.

The semi-final brought Real Madrid. Again! The two teams fought out a high quality 1-1 draw in the Bernabeu, setting up a tasty return leg at the Etihad. I travelled up to Manchester full of anticipation. Surely this year would be different?

The atmosphere at the Etihad was electric. Fireworks and blue smoke greeted the arrival of the team bus, and the noise before kick-off was unbelievable. Manchester City responded with the best 45 minutes football I've ever seen. Two goals from Bernardo Silva gave them a 2-0 half time lead, which would have been more but for a couple of athletic saves from Haaland by Courtois. City couldn't maintain that stratospheric standard in the second half, but still scored two more goals to finish 4-0 winners over the European champions. Unforgettably joyous and emotional scenes at the final whistle.

Now to source a ticket for the final! I had become superstitious about making any travel arrangements ahead of qualifying but on this occasion I booked accommodation using Holiday Inn loyalty points, and made a convoluted trip out via a pleasant evening in Budapest.

The day of the final was stinking hot, and the journey to the stadium was ghastly. I had headed into town to Taksim Square where there was live music and a huge replica trophy, then took the metro to catch the stadium transport for which there was an hour's queue. The bus journey was notionally one hour but took two through choking traffic, in the latter stages passing spectators who were jogging after being abandoned by their taxis. Istanbul is now the biggest city in Europe, and has suburbs the size of Bristol. Finally I reached the City fan zone at about 6pm, where there was a brilliant atmosphere – singing, beer, and good humour, with the worst of the heat having passed.

After a short walk I entered the stadium two hours before kick-off. I needed some food as I hadn't eaten for several hours and wasn't likely to for several more, so I joined a queue. It was an hour and a half before I was served, and had to make do with a barely edible 10 euro burger. I just made my seat behind one goal in time for kick-off. The Ataturk Olympic Stadium has, as its name suggests, an athletics track, so our view was not great.

After great semi-finals, finals are often an anti-climax, and as a spectacle this was no exception. The football was tense and City were nervy. For his second final running De Bruyne had to go off with an injury, though City's squad depth meant there was a more than able substitute in Foden. I had met up with an old friend Stewart, with whom I'd watched the famous Gillingham play-off 24 years earlier, and we sat together for the second half. Finally, after over an hour, Rodri broke the deadlock with a beautifully placed shot at our end. Inter Milan pressed hard and the last few minutes were very tense but at last the final whistle came, and we all experienced an adrenaline rush of pride and relief. Then the presentations in the middle distance, followed by a prolonged lap of honour and much joyful singing – 'we know who we are…' etc.

Mercifully the journey back into town wasn't so tortuous but it was still one o'clock when we reached Stewart's hotel, where we had a few beers and reminisced happily. Getting back to my hotel after 3 o'clock I found the bar still open and full of City fans. So I joined them for a couple more and, for the first time in at least 30 years, I finally got to bed after the sun had risen.

I flew straight home on the Monday, but City deservedly celebrated in style, flying back via a night in Ibiza. Jack Grealish had to be propped up at the Monday evening open top bus parade.

Reflections

L ooking back, I found my odyssey hard work but most interesting. As well as knowing my country better, I can now watch or read about a lower league match with some knowledge of the players and locations. I've particularly enjoyed the Sky Sports series about Salford City, 'The Class of 92'.

The standard of football has improved massively in recent years and I was pleasantly surprised by the skill levels in the lower divisions. I can remember when a 40 yard cross field pass to the feet of a winger would generate a round of applause. Now such a pass is commonplace, even in League Two, though the short goal kick hasn't really caught on in the lower divisions. The match experience has become much more commercialised, with clubs seizing the opportunity to sponsor substitutions, added time etc. And mercifully, stadium violence is now almost non-existent.

A couple of rants to the authorities:

Time keeping. Please, please can we just adopt a simple variation of the rugby system, whereby timekeeping is in the hands of a separate official, and the elapsed time is visible to all. The clock wouldn't be stopped every time the ball went out of play, just for injuries, substitutions, and VAR reviews. The current system is random and a joke. In most close matches the play from about 85 minutes is a dreary staccato jumble of time wasting, gamesmanship, and spurious unnecessary substitutions. And why not make full time when the ball goes out of play, rather than the unwritten arbitrary convention that the whistle doesn't go when a side is attacking?

Dissent. This seems more tolerated in England than overseas. The UK football authorities seem to regard screaming at the referee as part of the entertainment package. At every controversial decision the TV cameras zoom in on the aggrieved manager getting in the ear of the fourth official, who has had nothing to do with it. The Premier League recently announced that no more than two players could approach the referee, but after a couple of weeks has done nothing to enforce it. Many recreational leagues, including The Surrey Premier County League, where my son Adam plays, have adopted a ten minute sin bin penalty for dissent, and this has virtually eliminated the problem. Give it a try in the Football League. And perhaps for 'professional' fouls too? That would really change the match dynamics.

VAR. What more is there to be said? Personally, I would bin it, but that isn't going to happen. But if it's going to be retained, something must be done about communication. The people with least idea about what's going on are the spectators in the ground. I'd like to see referees miked up, as in rugby. The players would soon learn not to swear. But that probably won't happen either.

Eight months into the new season the Premier league looks more open than usual, with Manchester City, Liverpool and Arsenal in the race. Meanwhile Jude Bellingham and Harry Kane are making a big mark at Real Madrid and Bayern Munich respectively, and are the leading scorer in their leagues. There has been the usual managerial merry-go-round, with Wayne Rooney lasting only 83 days at Birmingham City. Alejandro Garnacho is fulfilling his promise and has probably already scored the goal of the season. At the other end of the age spectrum, Dean Lewington, in his 20th season at MK Dons, has overtaken the record of 771 appearances for a single club, previously held by Swindon's John Trollope. And at last we've had a female referee in the Premier League – Rebecca Welch.

Back in June, when I finally went to bed at dawn after the Champions League final, I knew that I had witnessed the apogee of over seven decades watching Manchester City. The treble was a once in a generation achievement, unlikely to be repeated. The squad had instantly moved on, with the departure of Gundogan and Mahrez. Winning a fourth consecutive Premier League feels a step too far, so I have confined my ambition for this season to retaining the Champions League. This would be very special, with the final being at Wembley.

Meanwhile the club has added another couple of trophies to its cabinet. In August I went to a sweltering hot Athens to see them beat Sevilla FC to win the European Super Cup. And in December they travelled to Saudi Arabia and won the World Club Championship. This may not be the most prestigious trophy, but it did confirm Manchester City as the best team on the planet. So as I write, they hold five trophies. They have given these a huge worldwide circulation, and recently allowed London based fans a memorable photo opportunity at an unlikely venue – The Horseshoe in Clerkenwell. This is probably a short-lived triumph, but we supporters could, for now at least, truthfully sing with pride the chant 'The Best Team in the Land and all the World'.

A friend recently told me that someone he knew had also just completed the 'All 92' (though not in one season), and was now moving on to the National League. But I think I'll pass on that, and just head hopefully to Germany this summer for Euro 2024.

May 2024